weekend knitting

50 UNIQUE PROJECTS AND IDEAS

Melanie Falick

Photographs by

Ericka McConnell

STC CRAFT | A MELANIE FALICK BOOK | NEW YORK

For Ben

Published in 2009 by
Stewart, Tabori & Chang
An imprint of Harry N. Abrams, Inc.

Originally published in hardcover in 2003
by Stewart, Tabori & Chang

Library of Congress Cataloging-in-Publication Data
Falick, Melanie
Weekend knitting : 50 unique projects and ideas / Melanie Falick;
photographs by Ericka McConnell
p. cm.
ISBN: 978-1-58479-769-2
1. Knitting--Patterns. I. Title
TT820.F17 2003
746.43'20432--dc21
2003054388

DESIGNED BY SUSI OBERHELMAN

The text of this book was composed in Bauer Bodoni and Avenir

Printed in Singapore

10 9 8 7 6 5 4 3 2 1

HNA
harry n. abrams, inc.
a subsidiary of La Martinière Groupe
115 West 18th Street
New York, NY 10011
www.hnabooks.com

contents

introduction

I often tell new knitters that knitting is nothing more than two stitches—knit and purl—and one is just the reverse of the other, so you could even say it is just one stitch. This statement usually makes them feel confident that they can learn. But the truth is that knitting can be so much more. Knitting, if you choose, can be at the heart of a fulfilling and creative way of living.

When you make time to knit, you make time for your own creativity, sitting still, and letting your mind wander. You experience the joy—and pride—of making something with your hands, feeling soft fibers, and watching beautiful colors run through your fingers. You meet new friends, many of whom see you through your knitting projects as well as life's ups and downs.

Although many of us squeeze in knitting time during the week, it is usually on the weekend that we can embrace our love for knitting most fully. If we're lucky, we can devote whole days to it. And if we choose small projects—or knit very quickly—we can finish a project in a single weekend. While instant gratification isn't always required, it is, at times, a satisfying counterpoint to much of what goes on in our typically busy lives. What fun it is to cast on for a scarf on Saturday morning and wrap it around our necks by Sunday night! Or to cast on for a bonnet while visiting friends who've just had a new baby—and then present them with the bonnet before the end of the stay.

While I was writing this book, I stopped and knitted my four-year-old son a pair of mittens. He requested that I make them and, in truth, I was reluctant at first because I was so busy. But once I started I realized that knitting was exactly what I needed. As I relaxed into the rhythm of the stitches, my mind stopped racing. As I focused on a single task, out of nowhere I seemed to come up with new ways of looking at other challenges. When the mittens were done after knitting for two short evenings, I felt a sense of completion. And, of course, each time I saw my son wearing his mittens, I knew it was my stitches and the love I knitted into them that were keeping his hands warm.

You can complete most of the projects in this book in a few weekends or less. Some may take a bit longer but were included because they fit into my idea of an idyllic weekend, one filled with fresh air, beautiful scenery, good friends, delicious food, laughter, and time to knit. While it's sometimes hard to pull together all of these elements at one time, it is often possible to achieve a few at once and to appreciate them when they happen. *Weekend Knitting* isn't just about Saturday and Sunday, just like knitting isn't just about two stitches. Both are a state of mind, a way to live.

ome and hearth

flower washcloths

CINDY TAYLOR

I knitted my first washcloth when a pattern for a round one sparked my interest. I didn't really think about using the washcloth. I just wanted to make something round, a shape I'd never tried to knit. Since then I have become a knitted-washcloth convert. At the end of a hectic day, I lather it up with soap, wash my face, and feel, at least for a moment, that I am doing something special for myself. It's amazing how something so seemingly inconsequential can actually have a profound effect (it nearly always compels me to take a deep, relaxing breath).

The flower shape of the cushy cotton chenille washcloths shown here is achieved in what you could call a reverse-bloom style: First you knit the five petals (blooms) in garter stitch, then you attach them to each other by knitting them together in the round; to finish, you work in Stockinette stitch, with gradual decreases, to the center.

This project can be worked entirely on double-pointed needles, but you can see the flower come to life nicely, and you can leave the petals on the circular needle as you complete them, if you begin with the circular needle and change to double-pointed needles when necessary.

Finished Measurements
10½" diameter, measured at widest point.

Yarn
Crystal Palace Cotton Chenille (100% cotton; 98 yards / 50 grams): 1 skein for each cloth. Shown in #6320 green, #2054 pink, and #2230 orange.

Needles
16" circular (circ) needle size US 6 (4 mm).
One set double-pointed needles (dpn) size US 6 (4 mm), longer than 8" recommended.
Change needle size if necessary to obtain the correct gauge.

Notions
Stitch marker, yarn needle, stitch holders or waste yarn (optional).

Gauge
16 sts and 26 rounds = 4" in Stockinette stitch (St st).

PETALS (make 5)
Using either circ or dpn, CO 11 sts.
ROW 1: Knit across all sts.
For Rows 2–20, slip the last st of every row as if to purl with yarn in front, to create a smooth edge for the petal.
ROW 2: Insert the tip of the right-hand needle between the first 2 sts on the left-hand needle, draw up a loop, and place it on the left-hand needle—1 st

increased. Knit across all sts, slipping the last st of the row as given above.

ROWS 3, 4, AND 5: Repeat Row 2—15 sts after completing Row 5.

ROWS 6 AND 7: Knit across all sts, slipping last st as before.

ROWS 8 AND 9: Repeat Row 2—17 sts after completing Row 9.

ROWS 10 AND 11: Knit across all sts, slipping last st as before.

ROWS 12 AND 13: Repeat Row 2—19 sts after completing Row 13.

ROWS 14 AND 15: Knit across all sts, slipping last st as before.

ROWS 16 AND 17: Repeat Row 2—21 sts after completing Row 17.

ROWS 18, 19, AND 20: Knit across all sts, slipping last st as before.

ROW 21: Knit across all sts.

Break yarn, leaving an 8" tail. Make 4 more petals for a total of 5

petals. If using a circ needle, you can leave the petals on the cable part of the needle as you work the others. If using dpns, place petals on stitch holders or waste yarn.

FLOWER CENTER

Place all petals on circ needle or dpns with the yarn tail hanging at the same side of each petal. Join for working in the rnd (round), and place marker to indicate the beginning of rnd—105 sts. If beginning on circ needle, change to dpns when there are too few sts to continue using the circ.

RNDS 1, 2, AND 3: Knit all sts.

RND 4: *K2, k2tog; repeat from * around to last st, end k1—79 sts.

RNDS 5 AND 6: Knit all sts.

RND 7: *K2, k2tog; repeat from * to last 3 sts, end k3—60 sts.

RND 8 AND 9: Knit all sts.

RND 10: *K2, k2tog; repeat from * to end—45 sts.

RNDS 11 AND 12: Knit all sts.

RND 13: *K2, k2tog; repeat from * to last st, end k1—34 sts.

RNDS 14 AND 15: Knit all sts.

RND 16: *K1, k2tog; repeat from * to last st, end k1—23 sts.

RND 17: Knit all sts.

RND 18: *K1, k2tog; repeat from * to last 2 sts, end k2tog—15 sts.

RND 19: Knit all sts.

RND 20: K2tog around to last st, end k1—8 sts.

RND 21: BO all sts.

Weave in ends securely, weaving each end back on itself to ensure that it does not work loose. To block, saturate with water, pat gently into shape, and allow to air-dry.

Let me warn you
that a genuine
interest in knitting
can keep you
fascinated, eagerly
pursuing it,
and never satisfied,
through a lifetime.

From *Woman's Day Book of American Needlework*, ROSE WILDER LANE, 1963

TAKING A Bath

A nice way to complete a relaxing weekend of knitting—or to begin one if it has been a stressful week—is to take a peaceful soak in the tub. With a little forethought and minimal effort, the bath can be made especially comforting. From the following list or your own imagination, pick and choose a few special touches that will help you make the experience serene.

- Clean the bathroom, especially the tub.

- If necessary, turn up the heat in the bathroom a few minutes before you start running the water.

- Light some candles and place them in areas of the bathroom where they are steady and will not fall.

- Place fresh flowers in a vase in a safe spot where you will be able to see them while you are in the tub.

- Choose a large, very soft bath towel to wrap yourself in after the bath, plus a smaller, equally soft towel for drying yourself off. Place the towels within arm's reach of the tub. If you are not planning a long bath, before you enter the bath, place the towels in the dryer to warm up for a few minutes.

- Place your most comfortable bathrobe and slippers or cozy socks in the bathroom.

- Turn off the ringer on the telephone.

- Play music that suits your mood. Choose music that will last at least as long as the bath. Check that the volume is at the level you like (without the noisy water running) before you get in the tub.

- Arrange a bath pillow in a comfortable spot in the tub.

- Place a sturdy chair or small bench within arm's reach of the tub. Place any small items you will need during the bath on the chair or bench. Consider a book, a journal and pen, a small knitting project, a beverage, and any special bath products you want to use.

- If desired, add bubble bath, bath salts, bath oils, flower petals, or other favorite bath products to the water.

- If other people are at home, ask not to be disturbed.

- Once you get in the tub, close your eyes and take some deep breaths to relax and clear your mind.

turtleneck egg cozies

KRISTIN NICHOLAS

Kristin Nicholas became interested in designing knitted soft-boiled egg sweaters—or cozies—after seeing one in *World of Interiors*, a toney British home-decorating magazine. Opposite is a Stockinette-stitch cozy. On page 17 are three other styles: garter stitch, seed stitch, and ribbed. If you find the idea of a sweater for your eggs too far-fetched, then make these as Christmas tree decorations or doll clothes, but before you nix the egg sweater idea completely, imagine sitting around the breakfast table with weekend guests and serving these up. They're sure to elicit, at the very least, a bit of interesting conversation or a lot of hearty laughter.

Basic Stockinette Cozy

Review notes on page 16 before beginning to knit. Shown in orange with light green and magenta flower, and light green with orange and magenta flower.

BACK AND FRONT

CO 15 sts and work in St st (see Notes) for 3½". On the next row, work neck opening as follows: Work 5 sts, sl (slip) next 5 sts to holder, using the backward loop method (see Notes) CO 5 sts for back of neck, work last 5 sts. Work even in St st until piece measures 7" from the beginning. BO all sts.

SLEEVES

Measure up 2" from bottom of sweater at both sides of front and back and place markers. Join yarn, and with RS facing, pick up and knit 12 sts between a pair of markers for sleeve. Work in St st for 3 rows, ending with a WS row. Decrease 1 st at each side of next row—10 sts. Work 3 rows even. Decrease 1 st at each side of next row—8 sts. Work even until sleeve measures 3½" from pickup row. BO all sts. Repeat for other sleeve.

Finished Measurements
Approximately 7" chest circumference and 3½" from bottom edge to shoulder.

Yarn
Harrisville Designs Highland 2-ply Worsted (100% wool; 200 yards / 100 grams): 1 skein will make approximately 6 solid-color cozies. Shown in #66 melon (orange), #38 teak (brown), #35 chianti (magenta), #8 hemlock (dark green), #7 tundra (light green), #14 woodsmoke (light teal)

Needles
One set straight needles size US 5 (3.75 mm).
One set double-pointed needles (dpn) size US 5 (3.75 mm) for neckband. Change needle size if necessary to obtain the correct gauge, although exact gauge is not essential for this project.

Notions
Stitch markers, stitch holders, yarn needle.

Gauge
16 sts and 27 rows = 4" in Stockinette stitch (St st).

notes

- The body of each cozy is worked from the lower front, up and over the shoulders, to the lower back. A neck opening is created at the shoulder line as you go.

- Stockinette Stitch in Rows (St st)
  ROW 1 AND ALL ODD-NUMBERED ROWS: (RS) Knit all sts.
  ROW 2 AND ALL EVEN-NUMBERED ROWS: (WS) Purl all sts.
  Repeat these 2 rows for pattern.

- Stockinette Stitch in Rounds (St st)
  ALL ROUNDS (RNDS): Knit all sts every rnd.

- K1, P1 Rib in the Round (even number of sts)
  ALL RNDS: *K1, p1; repeat from * to end.

- K2, P2 Rib (even number of sts)
  ROW OR RND 1: (RS) P3, *k2, p2; repeat from * to last 5 sts, end k2, p3.
  ROW OR RND 2: K3, *p2, k2; repeat from * to last 5 sts, end p2, k3.
  Repeat these 2 rows for pattern.

- Seed Stitch in Rows or Rounds (seed st)
  ROW 1: *K1, p1; repeat from *, ending k1 if there is an odd number of sts.
  ROW 2 AND ALL FOLLOWING ROWS OR ROUNDS: Purl the knit sts, and knit the purl sts as they appear.

- Backward Loop Cast-on: *Make a loop in the working yarn and place on the right-hand needle, oriented so that it doesn't unwind, to CO 1 st; repeat from * for rem sts to be CO.

- Embroidery Stitches

LAZY DAISY STITCH   **FRENCH KNOT**

NECKBAND

Join yarn at side of neck opening, ready to work the sts on the front holder. Using dpn, knit across 5 sts from holder, pick up and knit 1 st at side of neck opening, pick up and knit 5 sts across back of neck, pick up and knit 1 st at side of neck opening—12 sts. Join for working in the rnd (round) and place marker to indicate the beginning of rnd. Work in either k1, p1 rib (as shown on orange sweater) or St st in Rounds (see Notes, as shown on light green sweater) for 7 rnds. Purl one rnd. BO all sts as if to purl on next rnd.

FINISHING

Sew sleeve and side seams, reversing seam at lower end of sleeve for 1" for cuff. Fold up lower end of each sleeve for cuffs. If desired, embroider the front of cozy with a lazy daisy flower with French knot center (see diagrams in Notes). Weave in ends.

Striped Garter-Stitch Cozy

Worked in light (L) and dark (D) stripes, with contrasting (C) neckband; shown in light teal and brown stripes with magenta.

BACK AND FRONT

With L, CO 13 sts. Knit 1 row. Change to D. *Knit 2 rows D, knit 2 rows L; repeat from * until seven 2-row stripes of D have been completed. On the next row, work neck opening as follows: With L, k4, sl (slip) next 5 sts to holder, using the backward loop method (see Notes) CO 5 sts for back of neck, k4. Next row: Knit with L. Continue stripe pattern and

work even until seven 2-row stripes of D have been completed after the neck opening. Change to L and knit 1 row. With L, BO as if to knit on the next row.

SLEEVES

Measure up 8 stripes from bottom of sweater at both sides of front and back and place markers. Using L, with RS facing, pick up and knit 13 sts between a pair of markers for sleeve. Knit 1 row with L. Change to D and work even in 2-row garter st stripes for 4 rows, ending with a WS row. Continuing stripe pattern, decrease 1 st at each side of next row—11 sts. Work even until four 2-row stripes of D have been completed. Change to L and knit 1 row. With L, BO as if to knit on the next row. Repeat for other sleeve.

NECKBAND

Join C at side of neck opening, ready to work the sts on the front holder. Using dpn, knit across 5 sts from holder, pick up and knit 1 st at side of neck opening, pick up and knit 5 sts across back of neck, pick up and knit 1 st at side of neck opening—12 sts. Join for working in the rnd (round) and place marker to indicate the beginning of rnd. Work in St st in Rounds (see Notes) for 7 rnds. Purl one rnd. BO all sts as if to purl on next rnd.

FINISHING

Sew sleeve and side seams. Weave in ends.

A SOFT-BOILED EGG
For the Cozy

Turtleneck Egg Cozy designer Kristin Nicholas knows a lot about eggs thanks to the exotic chickens she raises in her backyard. She starts nearly every day, rain or shine, by walking out to the coop and collecting the eggs from the hens' nests. When I asked her how she makes her soft-boiled eggs, she started by giving me this interesting explanation about gauging an egg's freshness: When submerged in water, the freshest eggs will sink to the bottom and lay on their sides horizontally; as the eggs age, they will begin to "stand up" vertically; and a very old egg will rise to the surface and float.

1 or more fresh eggs
Water

Bring enough water to cover the egg(s) to a gentle boil in a saucepan that is large enough to hold the egg(s) without crowding. Using a clean, sharp sewing needle or pin, poke a hole through the broad end of each egg (this will keep the shells from cracking due to the pressure of the white expanding inside); it takes only a small amount of force to make the hole.

Place the egg(s) on a large spoon or other cupped utensil and gently lower into the boiling water (the idea is to keep the eggs from knocking against each other or the saucepan to prevent them from cracking from the contact). Cook for 3 to 4 minutes, depending on how runny you like the yoke. With the spoon, transfer to an egg cup and cover with a cozy to keep warm.

When ready to eat, remove the cozy and crack the egg shell horizontally (still in the cup) with a knife about ½" down from the top of the egg. Lift the top shell and with a spoon eat the white that is inside of it. Eat the remainder of the egg out of the shell in the cup.

Note: If you want to make a medium- or hard-boiled egg (generally not served in a cozy), boil the egg between 5 and 15 minutes. After removing the egg from the water, run it under cold water, then peel away the shell.

Ribbed Cozy

Shown in magenta and light teal.

BACK AND FRONT

CO 16 sts and work in k2, p2 rib (see Notes) for 3½". On the next row, work neck opening as follows: Work 5 sts, sl (slip) next 6 sts to holder, using the backward loop method (see Notes) CO 6 sts for back of neck, work last 5 sts. Work even in k2, p2 rib until piece measures 7" from the beginning. BO all sts in rib.

SLEEVES

Measure up 2" from bottom of sweater at both sides of front and back and place markers. Join yarn, and with RS facing, pick up and knit 12 sts between a pair of markers for sleeve. Work in seed st (see Notes) for 3 rows, ending with a WS row. Decrease 1 st at each side of next row—10 sts. Work 3 rows even. Decrease 1 st at each side of next row—8 sts. Work even until sleeve measures 2½" from pickup row. BO all sts. Repeat for other sleeve.

NECKBAND

Join yarn at side of neck opening, ready to work the sts on the front holder. Using dpn, knit across 6 sts from holder, then pick up and knit 6 sts across back of neck—12 sts. Join for working in the rnd (round) and place marker to indicate the beginning of rnd. Work in seed st for 1". BO all sts in pattern on next rnd.

FINISHING

Sew sleeve and side seams, reversing seam at lower end of sleeves for 1" for cuffs. Fold up lower end of each sleeve for cuffs. Weave in ends.

Seed-Stitch Cozy

Shown in dark green.

BACK AND FRONT

CO 15 sts and work in seed st (see Notes) for 3½". On the next row, work neck opening as follows: Work 5 sts, sl (slip) next 5 sts to holder, using the backward loop method (see Notes) CO 5 sts for back of neck, work last 5 sts. Work even in seed st until piece measures 7" from the beginning. BO all sts.

SLEEVES

Measure up 2" from bottom of sweater at both sides of front and back and place markers. Join yarn, and with RS facing, pick up and knit 13 sts between a pair of markers for sleeve. Work in seed st for 3 rows, ending with a WS row. Decrease 1 st at each side of next row—11 sts. Work 3 rows even. Decrease 1 st at each side of next row—9 sts. Work even until sleeve measures 2½" from pickup row. BO all sts. Repeat for other sleeve.

NECKBAND

Join yarn at side of neck opening, ready to work the sts on the front holder. Using dpn, knit across 5 sts from holder, pick up and knit 1 st at side of neck opening, pick up and knit 5 sts across back of neck, pick up and knit 1 st at side of neck opening—12 sts. Join for working in the rnd (round) and place marker to indicate the beginning of rnd. Work in St st in Rounds (see Notes) for 7 rnds. Purl one rnd. BO all sts as if to purl on next rnd.

FINISHING

Sew sleeve and side seams, reversing seam at lower end of sleeves for 1" for cuffs. Fold up lower end of each sleeve for cuffs. Weave in ends.

When Stephen arrived, they continued
to talk idly for a while, of plants and eccentricities;
Stephen described a peculiar array of knitted
pot plants which an aunt of his had created—you mean
knitted? Yes, I do mean knitted, green leaves,
white-edged purple flowers, sort of knitted begonias
in little pots with real earth, quite realistic
from a couple of yards away . . . .

From *The Radiant Way*, MARGARET DRABBLE, 1987

lap blanket

fluffy afghan or

NICKY EPSTEIN

When there's a mild chill in the air, a lap blanket is a comforting fix. Made by combining a fluffy mohair blend yarn with a smooth wool-llama yarn in a bold color like chartreuse, it can also be a fun decorating detail. The lap-blanket size is easy to finish in a weekend. For knitters wanting a bigger blanket (and happy to invest more than a weekend's worth of time), instructions for a larger afghan are also provided.

notes

- Instructions for lap blanket are given first; instructions for afghan are given in parentheses.

- **K1f&b:** Knit into front and back of same stitch to increase one stitch.

Finished Measurements
Lap blanket approximately 25" x 37" (afghan approximately 52" x 62").

Yarn
Classic Elite Bravo (40% rayon, 35% mohair, 13% silk, 6% wool, 6% nylon; 48 yards / 50 grams): 9 (28) skeins main color (MC).
Classic Elite Montera (50% llama, 50% wool; 127 yards / 100 grams): 1 (3) skeins contrast color (CC). Lap blanket shown in Bravo #3719 signs of spring and Montera #3887 pear.

Needles
One 29" circular (circ) size US 9 (5.5 mm).
One 29" circ size US 13 (9 mm).
Change needle size if necessary to obtain the correct gauge.

Notions
Yarn needle.

Gauge
Using larger needles and MC, 12 sts and 14 rows = 4" in Stockinette stitch (St st). Using smaller needles and CC, 11 sts and 24 rows = 4" in garter stitch, slightly stretched.

Using larger needles and MC, CO 104 (216) sts and work in St st (knit 1 row, purl 1 row) for 3", ending with a WS purl row. *Change to smaller needles and CC. Next row: (RS) K2tog all the way across—52 (108) sts. Knit 5 more rows. Change to larger needles and MC. Next row: (RS) K1f&b (see Notes) in every stitch across—104 (216) sts. Work in St st for 4", ending with a WS row. Repeat from * 5 (10) more times—104 (216) sts; piece measures approximately 33 (58)" from beginning. Repeat from * once more, working St st with MC for only 3" so the final St st section matches the beginning St st section. BO all sts. Weave in ends. Block lightly, if desired.

A KNITTING Film Festival

For a fun day of camaraderie and stitchwork, invite a group of friends to gather around and watch movies with knitting scenes. If you're really feeling festive, make it a slumber party. Set out popcorn, beverages, and basic knitting tools for guests who brought their projects but may have forgotten a necessary gadget. For knitters who didn't bring their projects, offer scrap yarn and needles, so they can cast on if they get the urge (or have them work on a guest knitting project/see page 129). The knitting scenes in these films tend to be brief (blink and you'll miss some), but still it's interesting to see how knitting is portrayed. If you can't find some of the older films in your local video store, try a mail-order source like Facets in Chicago (www.facetsvideo.com).

Chicago (2002)
In this Academy Award–winning musical, Richard Gere (as lawyer Billy Flynn) suggests to his client Renée Zellweger (as wannabe chorus girl Roxie Hart) that she make herself look innocent of murder by wearing a nunlike dress and knitting in court.

Harry Potter and the Chamber of Secrets (2002)
Knitting needles that knit on their own are among the magical effects Harry witnesses when he visits fellow wizard Ron Weasley at home. Based on the book by J. K. Rowling.

Frida (2002)
In this story about Mexican artist Frida Kahlo, Mia Maestro (as Frida's sister) knits while she waits for Salma Hayek (as Frida) to wake after a crippling bus accident.

America's Sweethearts (2001)
In this light romantic comedy, Julia Roberts (as Kiki) knits from the sidelines while her celebrity sister and her estranged husband give interviews to promote their new movie.

Shipping News (2001)
Julianne Moore (as Wavey) and Judi Dench (as Agnis) get one knitting scene apiece in this story about pain, renewal, and self-discovery in a small Newfoundland port town. Lots of handknits throughout. An adaptation of the Pulitzer Prize–winning novel by E. Annie Proulx.

Sweet November (2001)
A sticky-sweet romance in which a bohemian Charlize Theron (as Sara) chooses to emotionally rescue a different man each month—until November, when one of the men touches her heart. Theron knits in one scene; lots of yarn throughout.

Chicken Run (2000)
A hen named Babs knits continuously during this clay animation feature about a flock of chickens determined to fly the coop.

Wallace and Gromit Trilogy (1990s)
From the makers of *Chicken Run*, three clay animation shorts— *A Grand Day Out*; *The Wrong Trousers* (winner of 1993 Academy Award for Best Animated Short); and *A Close Shave* (winner of 1995 Academy Award)—that follow the madcap adventures of Wallace, an inventor, and his loyal canine sidekick, Gromit, an avid knitter. In *A Close Shave*, Wallace invents a machine that shears sheep and knits sweaters; he also falls in love with a yarn shop owner.

Idle Hands (1999)
A comedy-horror cross in which the devil takes possession of a slacker's hand. In order to ward the devil off, the slacker keeps his hands busy by knitting. Better suited to teenagers than adults.

Dancing at Lughnasa (1998)
In this bittersweet story of the emotional lives of a Roman Catholic family in 1930s Ireland, two of five sisters knit gloves for income. Based on the Tony Award–winning play by Brian Friel.

Antonia's Line (1996)
Unwed mothers knit while waiting out their pregnancies in this quirky, sweet, cerebral film from Denmark. Winner of Academy Award for best foreign film.

Bridges of Madison County (1995)
After a passionate affair with a globe-trotting photographer, a lonely farm wife (played by Meryl Streep) knits in front of the television set with her family. Based on James Waller's novel.

Little Women (1994)

In the most recent remake of this classic tearjerker Trini Alvarado (as Meg March) knits while her sister Winona Ryder (as Jo) performs one of her plays. Other types of needlework are glimpsed throughout. Based on the book by Louisa May Alcott.

Like Water for Chocolate (1993)

When Tita, the heroine of this mystical Mexican tale, is told her beloved will marry her sister, the subtitles read, "A black hole had entered her and let in the cold. She knitted and cried until she finished a quilt that covered her." Watch closely and you'll see Tita is really crocheting—there's a mistake in the translation—but the film is still likely to please. Based on the book by Laura Esquivel.

9½ Weeks (1986)

In several of the art-gallery scenes in this steamy cult classic, Kim Bassinger (as Elizabeth) recounts her erotic adventures while her roommate knits on huge bamboo needles.

Murder Ahoy (1964)

In this Agatha Christie classic, Margaret Rutherford (as Miss Marple) knits a sock while unraveling a muderous plot aboard a naval cadet training ship.

Breakfast at Tiffanys (1961)

Audrey Hepburn (as Holly Golightly) knits an out-of-control sweater, wondering if she has confused her knitting pattern with building plans. A romantic adaptation of Truman Capote's novella.

Phone Call from a Stranger (1952)

Bette Davis (as invalid Marie Hoke) knits a sock while telling a visiting stranger the bittersweet tale of her marriage.

Mister Lucky (1943)

Cary Grant (as gambler Joe Adams) knits as part of the war effort—or, really, to get the girl. One of the longest knitting scenes in all the movies listed here.

The Wizard of Oz (1939)

Clara Blandick (as Auntie Em), knitting in her rocking chair, is one of several characters Judy Garland (as Dorothy) sees from her window as she and Toto are carried in their house to Oz.

A Tale of Two Cities (1935)

In one of many film versions of this Dickens classic, Blanche Yurka (as Madame Defarge) is vengeful, searing, and intent on overthrowing the French aristocracy. She knits nearly nonstop—and with lightning-fast speed—in all her scenes.

lace-edged pillowcases

ALISSA BAPTISTA

Made by cutting a strip of fabric out of an ordinary pillowcase, then inserting a strip of knitted lace, this easy project makes almost any bed look welcoming. Treat yourself and your guests to these special cases and/or knit them as a shower, bridal, or housewarming gift. Two different inserts—a leaf pattern and a love braid—are shown.

Review notes on page 27 before beginning to knit.

LEAF PATTERN
CO 18 sts.

ROW 1: (RS) Sl 1, k2, yo, ssk (see Notes), k1, [yo, k2tog] twice, k5, yo, k2tog, k1.

ROW 2 AND ALL EVEN-NUMBERED ROWS: (WS) Sl 1, k2, yo, p2tog, p9, k1, yo, k2tog, k1.

ROW 3: Sl 1, k2, yo, ssk, k2, [yo, k2tog] twice, k4, yo, k2tog, k1.

ROW 5: Sl 1, k2, yo, ssk, k3, [yo, k2tog] twice, k3, yo, k2tog, k1.

ROW 7: Sl 1, k2, yo, ssk, k4, [yo, k2tog] twice, k2, yo, k2tog, k1.

ROW 9: Sl 1, k2, yo, ssk, k10, yo, k2tog, k1.

ROW 10: Repeat Row 2.

Repeat Rows 1 - 10 until piece measures about 4" longer than desired finished length. Cut yarn. Place live sts on a separate length of yarn and knot the ends of the holding yarn securely.

Finished Measurements
Leaf pattern insert 3½" wide.
Love braid insert 4¼" wide.

Yarn
Jaeger Siena (100% mercerized cotton; 151 yards / 50 grams): 1 ball per pillowcase. Shown in #401 white.

Needles
One set short straight or 2 double-pointed (dpn) needles size US 3 (3.25 mm).
Change needle size if necessary to obtain the correct gauge.

Notions
T-pins, yarn needle, spray or liquid starch, iron, sewer's marking chalk or pencil, sharp-pointed sewing needle and matching thread, purchased pillowcase(s). Optional: Quilter's ruler, rotary cutter and board.

Gauge
18 sts measures 3½" wide, and 20 rows (2 repeats) measures 3¼" long in leaf pattern after blocking. 22 sts measures 4¼" wide, and 28 rows (1 repeat) measures 4" long in love braid pattern after blocking.

LOVE BRAID PATTERN
CO 22 sts.

ROW 1 AND ALL ODD-NUMBERED ROWS: (WS) Purl.

ROW 2: (RS) K5, [yo, ssk] twice (see Notes), k3, [k2tog, yo] twice, k6.

Front to back: Love braid pattern, leaf pattern.

notes

- As each lace insert is knitted it will tend to curl up on itself. To make it easier to check row gauge, knit a swatch at least 5" long, then check the gauge over the center stitches.

- All sl (slipped) stitches are slipped as if to purl with yarn in back.

- **Yo (yarnover):** Bring yarn to the front and over the right-hand needle. Work the newly-created loop as a st on the next row.

- **Ssk (slip, slip, knit):** Sl the next 2 sts to right-hand needle one at a time as if to knit, pass them back to left-hand needle one at a time in their new orientation, and knit them together through the back of their loops.

- **Sssk (slip, slip, slip, knit):** Sl the next 3 sts to right-hand needle one at a time as if to knit, pass them back to left-hand needle one at a time in their new orientation, and knit them together through the back of their loops.

ROW 4: K3, [k2tog, yo] twice, k4, [k2tog, yo] twice, k1, yo, ssk, k4.

ROW 6: K2, [k2tog, yo] twice, k4, [k2tog, yo] twice, k1, [yo, ssk] twice, k3.

ROW 8: K1, [k2tog, yo] twice, k4, [k2tog, yo] twice, k3, [yo, ssk] twice, k2.

ROW 10: K3, [yo, ssk] twice, k1, [k2tog, yo] twice, k5, [yo, ssk] twice, k1.

ROW 12: K4, yo, ssk, yo, sssk (see Notes), yo, k2tog, yo, k4, [k2tog, yo] twice, k3.

ROW 14: K5, yo, ssk, yo, sssk, yo, k4, [k2tog, yo] twice, k4.

ROW 16: K6, [yo, ssk] twice, k3, [k2tog, yo] twice, k5.

ROW 18: K4, k2tog, yo, k1, [yo, ssk] twice, k4, [yo, ssk] twice, k3.

ROW 20: K3, [k2tog, yo] twice, k1, [yo, ssk] twice, k4, [yo, ssk] twice, k2.

ROW 22: K2, [k2tog, yo] twice, k3, [yo, ssk] twice, k4, [yo, ssk] twice, k1.

ROW 24: K1, [k2tog, yo] twice, k5, [yo, ssk] twice, k1, [k2tog, yo] twice, k3.

ROW 26: K3, [yo, ssk] twice, k4, yo, ssk, yo, k3tog, yo, k2tog, yo, k4.

ROW 28: K4, [yo, ssk] twice, k4, yo, k3tog, yo, k2tog, yo, k5.

Repeat Rows 1–28 until piece measures about 4" longer than desired finished length. Cut yarn. Place live sts on a separate length of yarn and knot the ends of the holding yarn securely.

PILLOWCASE INSERTS

Launder pillowcase, and as an aid for more accurate measuring, press pillowcase to remove all wrinkles. Measure the width of the pillowcase opening and multiply by 2 to get the length of the insert.

Work the insert pattern of your choice until piece measures 4" longer than desired finished length. Weave in loose ends. Pin the insert flat and straight using T-pins, press, and starch.

To create space for lace insert, measure down at least 2¼" from open edge of pillowcase, or ½" past the pillowcase hem, and draw a line with a quilter's ruler, if desired. Cut along this line with scissors or rotary cutter; pillowcase is now in two sections. Turn the cut edges of each piece under ¼", hem by hand, and press.

Pin lace insert between sections of pillowcase as shown, positioning CO edge of insert at pillow side seam. Carefully unravel any extra length of knitted lace as necessary, return live sts to needle and BO all sts, leaving a 16" tail. Using the tail and yarn needle, sew CO and BO edges of insert together. Hand-stitch each edge of lace insert to pillowcase between pillowcase sections as shown.

argyle slippers

DENYSE SPECKTOR

Whem traveling in Russia, I came across an interesting custom I believe is common in much of the East. There, upon entering a house, everyone takes off his or her shoes and puts on a pair of slippers. This makes most people comfortable and prevents dirt from being tracked into the house. Families generally keep their own slippers, as well as extras for visitors, close to the front door. I like the idea of adopting this custom as is or, in a slightly altered way, by placing slippers in the guest room so overnight visitors have something to put on their feet while getting ready for bed or early in the morning.

Review notes on page 30 before beginning to knit.

SLIPPER TOP (make 2)

Using smaller needles and MC, CO 39 (41, 45) sts. Working 1 edge st at each side (see Notes) work seed st over center 37 (39, 43) sts for 4 (6, 8) rows. Set up argyle pattern: Joining a new strand of yarn for each color change, work 1 edge st, work 1 (2, 4) st seed st with MC, work Row 1 of argyle slipper chart over center 35 sts, work 1 (2, 4) sts seed st with MC, work 1 edge st. Work even from chart, maintaining edge sts and seed st at each side, until Row 26 has been completed. On the next 5 rows, decrease 2 sts at each side inside the seed st sections as follows: Work 2 (3, 5) sts as established; ssk (see Notes) twice on RS rows, or p2tog twice on

Finished Sizes
To fit women's sizes small (medium, large), approximate shoe sizes 6½ - 7 (8 - 9, 9½ - 11) or men's approximate shoe sizes 5 - 5½ (7 - 8, 8½ - 10). Shown in pale fuchsia colorway size medium, and burgundy colorway size large.

Yarn
Paternayan Persian Wool (100% wool; 40 yards / 1 ounce): 4 skeins each main color (MC), and 1 skein each colors A, B, C, and D according to your chosen colorway (see Note on page 30).
Pale Fuchsia Colorway: MC #323 pale fuchsia, A #570 dark navy, B #564 light blue, C #320 plum, D #634 spring green.
Burgundy Colorway: MC #900 red, A #652 olive, B #832 orange, C #815 yellow, D #310 dark plum.

Needles
One set straight needles size US 3 (3.25 mm).
One set straight needles size US 5 (3.75 mm).
Change needle size if necessary to obtain the correct gauge.

Notions
Yarn needle, crochet hook size D (3.25 mm), 12" of ¼" wide elastic, fabric glue, pair of purchased leather slipper soles in appropriate size (see Sources, page 175).

Gauge
Using smaller needles and two 2-ply yarn strands, 28 sts and 36 rows = 4" (10 cm) in Stockinette stitch (St st) argyle pattern from chart.

notes

- The yarn for this project is made up of three 2-ply strands. Separate a length of yarn into its individual 2-ply strands, and work with two of these strands held together in order to achieve the correct gauge.

- The argyle pattern is worked in Stockinette stitch intarsia, with sections worked in the main color at each side to achieve the different sizes. Use separate lengths of yarn for each argyle color section, twisting the yarns at each color change to avoid making a hole. Do not carry unused colors along the back of the work.

- **Seed Stitch (even number of stitches)**
  ROW 1: *K1, p1; repeat from * to end.
  ROW 2: *P1, k1; repeat from * to end.
  Repeat these 2 rows for pattern.

- **Seed Stitch (odd number of stitches)**
  ALL ROWS: *K1, p1; repeat from * to last st, end k1.

- **Edge Stitches:** Sl (slip) the first stitch of each row as if to purl with yarn in back; knit the last stitch of each row through back of loop.

- **Ssk (slip, slip, knit):** Sl the next 2 sts to right-hand needle one at a time as if to knit, pass them back to left-hand needle one at a time in their new orientation, and knit them together through the back of their loops.

- **Sssk (slip, slip, slip, knit):** Sl the next 3 sts to right-hand needle one at a time as if to knit, pass them back to left-hand needle one at a time in their new orientation, and knit them together through the back of their loops.

ARGYLE SLIPPER CHART

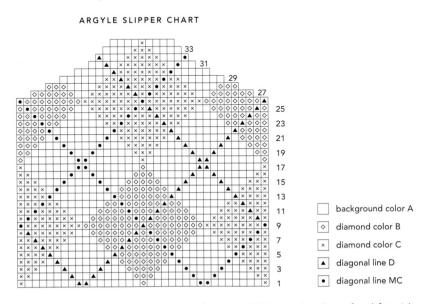

- □ background color A
- ◇ diamond color B
- × diamond color C
- ▲ diagonal line D
- • diagonal line MC

Work RS (odd-numbered) rows from right to left, and work WS (un-numbered) rows from left to right.

WS rows; work to last 4 sts of argyle pattern; k2tog twice on RS rows, or ssp (see Notes) twice on WS rows; work last 2 (3, 5) sts as established— 19 (21, 25) sts remain when Row 31 has been completed; 15 argyle sts from chart; 2 (3, 5) sts outside chart pattern at each side. On the next 3 rows, decrease 1 st at each side inside the seed st sections as follows: Work 2 (3, 5) sts as established; ssk on RS rows, p2tog on WS rows; work to last 2 sts of argyle pattern; k2tog on RS rows or ssp on WS rows; work last 2 (3, 5) sts as established—13 (15, 19) sts remain when Row 34 has been completed; 9 argyle sts from chart; 2 (3, 5) sts outside chart pattern at each side. Break off all colors except MC. Work 3 (4, 5) rows seed st across all sts, then BO all sts. Weave in all ends.

INTERIOR SOLE BANDS (make 2)

Using larger needles and MC, CO 5 sts. Maintaining the first and last sts as edge sts, work in seed st until band, slightly stretched, fits all the way around the inside of leather sole opening. BO all sts. Sew CO and BO ends together. Weave in ends.

EXTERIOR SIDE BANDS (make 2)

Using larger needles and MC, CO 7 sts. Maintaining the first and last sts as edge sts, work in seed st until band, slightly stretched, fits all the way around the outside of leather slipper sole opening. BO all sts. Sew CO and BO ends together. Weave in ends.

FINISHING

Block slipper tops lightly to even out the sts. Sew slipper tops to exterior bands, positioning seam at the center back heel. Temporarily place the assembled pieces on the slipper sole, making sure that the slipper top is correctly positioned on the sole, and mark the center of the exterior seed st band on each side of leather sole. Remove assembled pieces from leather sole. Cut elastic slightly shorter than the width of slipper instep. Glue elastic to marked positions at each side of leather sole, using fabric glue. Stretch and glue interior band to inside of sole opening, positioning seam at center back heel. Stretch and glue exterior band to outside of opening. Sew exterior and interior bands together along top edge, leaving a space for the elastic to emerge. Using MC and yarn needle, sew lower edge of exterior band to sole through holes provided, sewing twice around in an "X" pattern as given in sole instructions.

For now she need not think about anybody.
She could be herself. And that was what now, she often
felt the need of—to think; well not even to think.
To be silent; to be alone. All the being and the doing,
expansive, glittering, vocal, evaporated . . .
Although she continued to knit, and sat upright, it was
thus that she felt herself; and this self having
shed its attachments was free for the strangest adventures.

From *To the Lighthouse*, VIRGINIA WOOLF, 1927

diamond chair cushions

KRISTIN NICHOLAS

Kristin Nicholas designed these colorful cushions for her home, which is brimming with bold knitting like this as well as her paintings and pottery. We originally envisioned one colorway for fall/winter and one for spring/summer but, as it turned out, the cushions look terrific together.

Review notes on page 34 before beginning to knit.

CUSHION FRONT

Using larger needles and MC, CO 57 sts. Work in stranded-colorwork St st from chart using MC and CC as indicated, increasing 1 st at each side on Row 15, then every 10 rows 5 more times as shown—69 sts. Work even until Row 73 of chart has been completed. BO all sts using MC.

EDGING

Use 3 circ needles to work the edging: 2 needles to hold the sts for 4 sides, and a third needle for working the sts. Alternatively, use a single, very long circ needle to hold sts from all 4 sides.

PICKUP RND (ROUND): Using magenta and smaller circ needles for both versions, with RS facing and beginning at the right side of CO edge, pick up and knit 57 sts along CO, pm (place marker) pick up 1 st in corner, pm, pick up and knit 50 sts along the side of the cushion at a rate of approximately 2 sts for every 3

Finished Measurements
Approximately 17½" wide across front edge, 14½" wide across back edge, and 16½" deep from front to back, including edging.

Yarn
Classic Elite Yarns Montera (50% llama, 50% wool; 127 yards / 100 grams): 2 skeins main color (MC), 2 skeins contrast color (CC), 1 skein each of 2 edging colors according to your chosen colorway.
Autumn Cushion: MC #3885 orange, CC #3827 cochineal, #3832 magenta and #3881 lima green for edging.
Spring Cushion: MC #3887 pear green, CC #3872 light teal, #3832 magenta and #3885 orange for edging.

Needles
One set straight needles size US 9 (5.5 mm) straight needles or 24" circular (circ) needle for cushion front.
Three 24" or longer circ needles size US 7 (4.5 mm) for edging.
Change needle size if necessary to obtain the correct gauge.

Notions
Stitch markers, yarn needle, 1 piece of 1" foam approximately 18" x 16" for each cushion, ½ yard 45" fabric for each cushion back, sharp-pointed sewing needle and matching sewing thread, crochet hook size L (8 mm) for making ties.

Gauge
Using larger needles, 18 sts and 20 rows = 4", in stranded-colorwork Stockinette stitch (St st) in pattern from chart.

Depending on desired effect, knit cushions in the same or contrasting colorways. The Perfect Pie Shawl (page 84) hangs from the chair on right.

notes

- To make slightly smaller cushions, here are two suggestions: Knit with smaller needles to get a tighter gauge; each ¼-stitch more per inch in your new gauge will translate to about a ½-inch less in cushion width and length. Or continue working at the given gauge, but reduce the number of stitches and rows in the chart by drawing a new outline inside the original chart; every 5 stitches and 5 rows removed will translate to approximately 1" less in cushion width and length. Try to keep the pattern symmetrical, and if you decide to alter the outline of the chart, make sure to pick up correspondingly fewer stitches around the cushion front when working the edging.

- **M1 (Make 1):** With the tip of the left-hand needle inserted from front to back, lift the strand between the two needles onto the left-hand needle and knit it through the back of loop to increase 1.

- **Crochet Chain Stitch:** Make a slipknot and place on crochet hook. *Yarn over hook and draw through loop on hook; repeat from * for desired length.

> Have nothing
> in your house that
> you do not know
> to be useful or
> believe to be beautiful.
>
> WILLIAM MORRIS

rows (pick up in two consecutive rows, then skip one row, fudging when necessary to get to 50 sts), pm, pick up 1 st in corner, pm, pick up and knit 69 sts along front edge of cushion, pm, pick up 1 st in corner, pm, pick up and knit 50 sts along other side cushion as before, pm, pick up 1 st in corner, pm—230 sts.

RND 1: With magenta, purl all sts.

RND 2: Change to lima green for autumn cushion, or pear green for spring cushion. *Knit to marker, M1 (see Notes), slip marker, knit corner st, slip marker, M1; repeat from * three more times. Place a different-colored marker after the last st to indicate end of rnd—8 sts increased

(2 at each corner), 238 sts total.

RND 3: With lima green for autumn cushion, or pear green for spring cushion, purl all sts.

RND 4: Change to orange for both versions. *Knit to marker, M1, slip marker, knit corner st, slip marker, M1; repeat from * three more times, knit to end—8 sts increased, 246 sts total.

RND 5: With orange, purl all sts.

RND 6: Change to cochineal for autumn cushion, or light teal for spring cushion. Repeat Rnd 4—8 sts increased, 254 sts total.

RND 7: With cochineal for autumn cushion, or light teal for spring cushion, BO all sts as if to purl.

BACKING AND STUFFING

Weave in all ends. Block cushion front lightly to even out the sts. Using the cushion front as a template, cut a piece of backing fabric ½" bigger than cushion front all the way around. Fold under ½" around all sides of backing fabric and press. Using the cushion front as a template again, cut the foam exactly in the shape of the cushion front. Hand-sew backing to cushion front around the two sides and the back, leaving the wider front edge open. Insert the foam into the cushion and sew the front edge closed.

TIES

Using crochet hook and 1 strand each of MC and CC held together, make two 12" ties for each cushion using crochet chain stitch (see Notes), leaving a 4" tail at each end of both ties. Attach the center of each tie securely to a back corner of the cushion.

DIAMOND CUSHION

73
71
69
67
65
63
61
59
57
55
53
51
49
47
45
46
41
39
37
35
33
31
29
27
25
23
21
19
17
15
13
11
9
7
5
3
1

Work RS (odd-numbered) rows from right to left, and work WS (un-numbered) rows from left to right.

☐ main color (MC)

☒ contrast color (CC)

willow-lace chair seat

ANNIE MODESITT

Yes, you can actually sit on this chair, and you need not be dainty about it. Made out of nylon twine from the hardware store, the seat is very sturdy and unlikely to stretch. Although if it does, there is a solution: Pour boiling water over it, which will shrink the nylon. Designer Annie Modesitt likes to knit seats for chairs she finds at yard sales, which means oftentimes she can complete the project, including all of the materials, for under twenty dollars. The pattern includes instructions for adapting the seat for chairs of different sizes since, when you're relying on yard sales for your materials, you can't be too picky about dimensions.

Review notes on page 38 before beginning to knit.

GENERAL INSTRUCTIONS

Chair seats come in three basic shapes: regular squares or rectangles, slightly tapered trapezoids, and severely tapered trapezoids. The amount of tapering affects the rate of increasing or decreasing to shape the chair seat. In order to make the correct seat for your type of chair, measure the lengths across the back and front of the seat area, called the back support and front support. If the back and front support measurements are the same, you have a square or rectangular chair seat area, which we will call Type A.

If the measurements are different, divide the narrower back

Finished Measurements
For chair shown, seat measures approximately 11" wide across the back support rail, 10" deep at each side, and 16" wide across the front support rail. Your own chair will determine the measurements for your project.

Twine
For chair shown, #36 or 36-ply White Twisted Nylon Seine Twine (100% nylon; amount per spool varies by manufacturer, available from hardware stores): approximately 360 yards will be sufficient for most chair seats.

Needles
For chair shown, one set straight needles size US 10 (6 mm). Change needle size if necessary to obtain the correct gauge.

Notions
Stitch markers, T-pins, large curved darning needle with eye to fit twine (Chibi brand suggested, available from sewing supply stores), cable needle (cn) clothespins or tape (optional).

Gauge
For chair shown, 13 stitches and 15 rows = 4", or 3.25 stitches and 3.75 rows = 1", in Stockinette stitch (St st). The correct gauge for your project should be determined by swatching.

notes

- **Cable Cast-On**: *Insert the tip of the right-hand needle into the space between the last 2 sts on the left-hand needle and draw up a loop. Place the loop on the left-hand needle. Repeat from * until you have the required number of sts cast on. Try to work loosely and evenly.

- **Yo (yarnover)**: Bring twine to the front and over the right-hand needle. Work the newly-created loop as a st on the next row.

- **Right Twist (RT)**: Knit into the front loop of the second stitch on left-hand needle but do not remove it from needle, then knit into the first stitch on left-hand needle and slip both stitches off together.

- **2/2LC (left-crossing cable, worked 2 sts over 2 sts)**: Slip the next 2 sts to cn and hold in front, k2, k2 from cn.

- **2/2RC (right-crossing cable, worked 2 sts over 2 sts)**: Slip the next 2 sts to cn and hold in back, k2, k2 from cn.

- **Ssk (slip, slip, knit)**: Sl the next 2 sts to right-hand needle one at a time as if to knit, pass them back to left-hand needle one at a time in their new orientation, and knit them together through the back of their loops.

- **Sssk (slip, slip, slip, knit)**: Sl the next 3 sts to right-hand needle one at a time as if to knit, pass them back to left-hand needle one at a time in their new orientation, and knit them together through the back of their loops.

length by the wider front length. If the resulting number is between 0.50 and 0.85, you have a slightly tapered trapezoid, which we will call Type B. This is the most common type of chair seat. If the resulting number is between 0.85 and 1.0, treat the chair seat as Type A. If the back length divided by the front length is less than 0.50, you have a severely tapered trapezoid, which we will call Type C.

PLANNING YOUR PROJECT

You can use any strong, non-stretching fiber for the chair seat, but 36-ply nylon twine or 16-ply heavy cotton twine seems to work best. It doesn't matter what gauge you get as long as you make a swatch and use your gauge to determine the number of stitches to cast on and how many rows to work.

To determine how many sts to cast on, multiply the back support length by the number of sts per inch in your gauge swatch. Round the result up to the nearest even number.

For the chair shown, the back support length is 11 inches, and the gauge is 3.25 sts per inch. 11 inches multiplied by the gauge of 3.25 equals 35.75 sts. Rounded up to the nearest even number is 36 sts. Calculate the cast-on number for your own chair seat in this manner.

The charted willow lace pattern begins as a panel 28 sts wide and is worked over the center sts of the chair seat. For straight Type A seats, the lace pattern maintains the same number of sts throughout, with no shaping. For tapered Type B and C seats, the number of sts in the lace panel will increase and decrease as described below, in order to accommodate the shape of the chair seat.

WILLOW LACE CHART

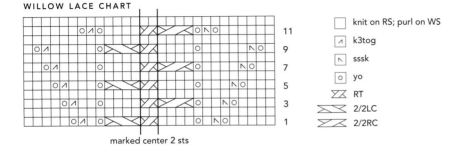

marked center 2 sts

	Symbol
□	knit on RS; purl on WS
↗	k3tog
⋏	sssk
○	yo
⤬	RT
⤬	2/2LC
⤬	2/2RC

Work RS (odd-numbered) rows from right to left, and work WS (un-numbered) rows from left to right.

Sts outside the lace pattern at each side are worked in St st (knit all sts on RS rows, purl all sts on WS rows). Subtract the 28 sts of the chart from your cast-on number of sts, and divide the result by 2. This number is how many sts to work in St st, on either side of the lace pattern.

For the chair shown, 36 cast-on sts, minus 28 sts for the lace chart, divided by 2, equals 4 sts to be worked in St st at each side of chart. Calculate the number of sts to work in St st at each side of the lace panel for your own chair seat in this manner.

To determine how many rows to work for the seat center, multiply the side support length by the number of rows per inch in your gauge swatch. Round up to the nearest whole number.

For the chair shown, the side support length is 10 inches, and the gauge is 3.75 rows per inch. 10 inches multiplied by 3.75 equals 37.5 rows. Rounded up to the nearest whole number is 38 rows. Calculate the number of rows for the center of your chair seat in this manner.

To determine how many sts you will need across the front support, multiply the front support length by the number of sts per inch in your gauge swatch. Round up to the nearest even number. For straight Type A chairs, the number remains the same throughout.

For the chair shown, the front support length is 16 inches. 16 inches multiplied by the gauge of 3.25 sts per inch is 52 sts. This number does not need to be rounded up to the nearest even number, but your number might. Calculate the number of sts you need across the front support for your own chair in this manner.

Knitting the Seat

BACK EXTENSION

CO the number of sts required for your chair seat. First row: (RS) Work the number of sts required outside the charted lace pattern in St st, pm (place marker), work Row 1 of willow lace pattern from chart over center 28 sts, pm, work in St st to end. Work even in pattern as established until piece measures 2½", ending with a RS row, and placing markers on either side of the center 2 cable sts in the last row. Beginning with the next row you will CO 2½" worth of sts at each end for side extensions.

For the seat shown, 2½ inches multiplied by 3.25 equals 8.125, so we cast on 8 sts at each side. Multiply your gauge per inch to determine the number of sts to CO for your chair. Transfer the needle with the sts to your left hand, pm, and use the cable cast-on method (see Notes) to CO 2½" worth of sts. Next row (WS) Purl the new CO sts

for side extension, sl m (slip marker), work in pattern to end of row, pm, transfer needle with sts to left hand, and CO 2½" worth of sts for other side extension. Work the side extension sts in St st throughout.

SEAT CENTER

For the next section, you will work in pattern as established for the number of rows required for the seat center, increasing 1 st on either side of the marked center cable for Types B and C. If you have a Type A seat, work this section even throughout, with no increases on either side of the center cable.

In order to determine how often to work the paired yo (see Notes) increases, subtract the number of sts across the back support from the number of sts needed across the front support; do not include the side extension sts in this calculation. This is the number of sts you need to increase. Because there are 2 yo's worked in every increase row, divide

the number of extra sts needed by 2 to get the number of increase rows.

For the chair shown, the number of sts needed across the front support is 52, and the number of sts across the back support is 36. Subtracting the back number from the front, we need to increase 16 sts. 16 sts divided by 2 equals 8 increase rows. Calculate the number of increase rows for your own chair seat in this manner.

Plan the spacing of the increase rows as evenly as possible over the length of the seat center, but don't worry if they are not exactly even. The process of stretching the knitted seat over the chair frame will help the seat conform to the shape of the chair. You may work some rows without shaping at each end of the seat center if it will help average out the increase intervals.

For the chair shown, the seat center is 38 rows long, and we needed a total of 8 increase rows; 38 divided by 8 equals 4.75 rows, which is, of course, not possible. However, we can arrange the increases every 4th row, and one way of doing this is as follows: Work 5 rows even, [increase in next row, work 3 rows even] 7 times, increase in next row, work 4 rows even—8 increase rows, 38 rows total. Calculate the spacing of the increase rows for your own chair in this manner.

For Type B and C chair seats, work each increase row as follows: Work in pattern to m before center 2 sts, yo, sl m, work center 2 sts, sl m, yo, work in pattern to end—2 sts increased. On the following row, work yo increases in St st. To make it easier to continue following the charted lace pattern as the number of sts increases, you may find it helpful to set off the increased sts with markers, and remember to work them in St st.

After working the increases required by Types B and C, the number of sts in the center section (not counting the side extensions) should equal the number of sts needed across the front support. For Type A, this will be the same number as across the back support (not counting the side extensions). Work even if necessary until the required number of rows for the seat center have been completed.

FRONT EXTENSION
At the beginning of the next 2 rows, BO the side extension sts, removing their markers. Work even in pattern as established until piece measures 2½" from side extension bind-offs.

SEAT UNDERSIDE
Discontinue lace pattern, but retain the center cable m, and work in St st for the same number of rows as required for the seat center. *At the same time,* make decreases at the same intervals as the seat center increases as foll: Work to 2 sts before first m, work 2 sts tog (together), sl m, work 2

center sts, sl m, work 2 sts tog, work to end. When all decreases and rows have been completed you should have the same number of sts as originally cast-on. BO all sts loosely, leaving a 2- to 3-foot tail for seaming.

ASSEMBLY
Position the chair seat on the chair, with the RS of lace-patterned seat center on top, the seat underside hanging down in front, and the side extensions hanging down at each side. If desired, use clothespins or tape to hold the seat in place temporarily. Turn the chair upside-down and rest it on the edge of a table. Pull the seat underside around the front support so the CO and BO edges meet. Using a curved darning needle and the long tail, sew the CO and BO edges together, stitch-for-stitch. Pull the seam tight every few sts and aim for a uniform look. Cut twine and weave in end.

Pull side extensions smoothly around the side supports and pin to seat underside. Sewing the side extensions is the most challenging part of this project. It can be helpful to start a length of sewing twine at each side and work both sides at once, sewing a few sts at a time from each side, switching from side to side to maintain uniform tension in the chair seat. Cut twine and weave in ends. The seat will feel taut at this point, but not as tight as it will need to be for use. You still need to block the chair seat and shrink the fiber.

BLOCKING
Set chair in tub or sink and carefully pour very hot (nearly boiling) water over seat to draw it up firmly and tightly. Air-dry.

The world of reality has its limits;

the world of imagination is boundless.

JEAN-JACQUES ROUSSEAU

It happens often. We find a special yarn—in a ball, hank, or skein—and think how pretty it looks and feels. But then we inevitably ask ourselves, What can I make with this? Rather than right away focusing on how to transform a yarn into a sweater, socks, or something else, sometimes it's nice to simply enjoy its natural beauty. Here are some ideas for creative ways to display yarn around the house—indefinitely or until some later date when a perfect project reveals itself. Oftentimes just looking at a particularly beautiful yarn is inspiring and uplifting, in the same way that a painting, photograph, or vase of flowers can be.

- Place pretty colors together in clean wooden bowls, natural baskets, boxes, buckets, or other types of creative holders. Scour yard sales and antique shops for unusual choices. Casually combining an assortment of colors often leads to new discoveries about how colors play off one another.

- "Dress" a vintage dress form in yarn. Drape yarn across its shoulders, or around its neck or waist.

- Drape yarn around the back of a chair or on the door of a cabinet or armoire.

- Fill an armoire with yarn and leave doors open to display.

- Use a hank of yarn as a curtain tie-back.

- Hang different colors of yarn on the pegs of a coat rack.

- String an assortment of yarn on a cord and hang from a wall hook.

- Line up cones of yarn on a shelf.

- Set up shelves or cubbies along an entire wall and arrange the yarn in a pleasing sequence of colors and textures. While some knitters will do this in a storage or workroom, it can also work well in a more public space.

- If you like to paint, draw, or take photos, consider using your yarn as a subject for a still life.

floral-oat pillow pair

JO SHARP

If ever there is a time for throw pillows, it's weekends. Toss these two on the couch, on the hammock, or at the back of a big, cushy armchair, then lean back and relax.

Finished Measurements
Approximately 18" square.

Yarn
Jo Sharp Silkroad Aran Tweed (85% wool, 10% silk, 5% cashmere; 104 yards / 50 grams)

Solid Pillow
#122 beach (oatmeal), 4 skeins.

Floral Pillow
#113 russet (dark brown), 3 skeins. #122 beach (oatmeal), #121 brindle (gray), and #119 licorice (black), 1 skein each.

Needles
One set straight needles size US 8 (5 mm). Change needle size if necessary to obtain the correct gauge.

Notions
Yarn needle, 18" square knife-edge pillow form for each pillow, four 7/8" buttons for each pillow.

Gauge
18 sts and 24 rows = 4" in Stockinette stitch (St st).

UPPER FRONT **Both Versions**
Using beach for solid version, or russet for floral version, CO 81 sts and work in St st for 6¾", ending with a WS (purl) row. Change to garter st (knit all sts every row) and work for 10 rows (5 garter ridges), ending with a WS row. Buttonhole row: (RS) K17, *BO 2 sts, k12 (13 sts on needle in this section); repeat from * two more times, BO 2 sts, k16 (17 sts on needle in last section). Next row: *Knit to gap created by BO in previous row, CO 2 sts; repeat from * three more times, knit to end. Knit every row until garter st section measures 3" high (approximately12 garter ridges total), ending with a WS row. BO all sts on next row as if to knit.

LOWER FRONT **Both Versions**
Using beach for solid version, or russet for floral version, CO 81 sts and work in St st for 10¾". BO all sts.

BACK **Solid Version**
Using beach, CO 81 sts and work in St st until piece measures 18". BO all sts.

BACK **Floral Version**
Using russet, CO 81 sts and work in St st intarsia from chart until Row 108 of chart has been completed. Use separate lenths of yarn for each color section, twisting the yarns at each

color change to avoid making holes. Do not carry unused colors along the back of the work. BO all sts using russet.

FINISHING

Weave in ends. Press all pieces gently on WS using a warm iron over a damp cloth. Place garter st section of the upper front over the lower front, overlapping the pieces approximately 2½" to form an 18" square. Baste the pieces together at the sides. Mark the placement of 4 buttons underneath the buttonholes and sew on buttons. With right sides together, sew front and back together around all 4 sides. Turn piece right side out and insert pillow form through front opening. Button closed.

In the midst of complexity, handicrafts provide simplicity. In the midst of movement and noise, they make space for silence and solitude.

SUSAN LYDON

Work RS (odd-numbered) rows from right to left, and work WS (un-numbered) rows from left to right.

farmer's market bag

PAM ALLEN

Good-bye plastic bags. Take this oversized carryall to the weekend farmer's market and fill it up in style and in good conscience (knowing you are doing your part to protect our planet). Because the bag is knitted very large then felted down to size, the knitted fabric is dense and strong enough to hold a lot of weight. Because the bag is worked on large (size 11) needles with bulky yarn, the striking geometric pattern comes to life quickly. The background is worked in two similar reddish-orange colors, creating a very subtle striping, similar to the *abrash* effect on Asian carpets woven with naturally-dyed yarns that are never exactly the same color from skein to skein.

Finished Measurements
Approximately 16" wide x 18" high, after felting, not including handles.

Yarn
Classic Elite Yarns Montera (50% llama, 50% wool; 127 yards / 100 grams): Color A, 4 skeins; colors B, C, and D, 1 skein each. Shown in A #3842 basilico (purple), B #3853 black cherry (dark wine-red), C #3868 orange, and D #3821 sage.

Needles
One set of five 10" double-pointed needles (dpn) size US 11 (8 mm). One 29" circular (circ) needle size US 11 (8 mm).

Notions
Stitch holders, stitch marker, yarn needle.

Gauge
14 sts and 16 rounds = 4" in stranded colorwork Stockinette stitch (St st) before felting. Because the bag will be felted, exact gauge is not critical.

Review notes on page 48 before beginning to knit.

BASE
Using dpn and A, CO 13 sts.
ROWS 1 AND 2: Knit with color A.
ROWS 3 AND 4: Knit with color B.
Repeat Rows 1–4 twenty-eight more times. There will be 58 2-row stripes (29 stripes each of A and B), ending with a stripe in color B. Work Rows 1–2 once more—59 stripes total. BO all sts.

BAG
With dpn and A, pick up and knit 11 sts along narrow end of striped base, with a second dpn pick up and knit 55 sts along side edge of base, with a third dpn pick up and knit 11 sts along second narrow end of base, and with a fourth dpn pick up and knit 55 sts along rem side edge—132 sts. Join for working in the rnd (round) and place marker for beginning of rnd. Beginning with Rnd 1 of chart, work 22-st repeat of chart 6 times around. Alternating between colors B and C every 10–12 rnds (a 10- to 12-rnd stripe of B, followed by a 10- to 12-rnd stripe of C), work Rnds

checkers travel sets

SHEILA MEYER

Board games are universally appealing and oftentimes bridge gaps between generations and even cultures, making it possible for people who don't think they have anything to share to find common ground. Knit these boards—and their accompanying bags—and take them to a local café or on vacation for hours of fun. Both sets are made with machine-washable yarn. The checker set is knitted in cotton and the backgammon set is knitted in wool, but the yarns—because they work up at the exact same gauge—are interchangeable. The backgammon bag can be carried with the board attached on the outside (as shown at right) or with the board rolled up inside. The checkers set (shown on pages 55 and 56) includes instructions for a large drawstring bag to hold the board and a small drawstring bag to hold the pieces. Review notes on page 52 before beginning to knit either project.

Backgammon Tote

BACK

Using pistachio, CO 91 sts. Work in cartridge belt rib (see Notes) until piece measures 15". Buttonhole row: Work 44 sts in pattern, BO center 3 sts for buttonhole, work in pattern to end. On the next row, CO 3 sts over gap in previous row to complete buttonhole. Work even in pattern until piece measures 17". BO all sts.

FRONT

Work same as back until piece measures 12½". BO all sts.

BACKGAMMON

Finished Measurements
Tote: Approximately 14" square, excluding handle and flap closure.
Board: 19" long and 10" wide, excluding ties.

Yarn
Mission Falls 1824 Wool (100% wool; 85 yards / 50 grams): #028 pistachio, 10 skeins; #011 poppy, 2 skeins; #021 denim, 1 skein.

Needles
One set straight needles size US 7 (4.5 mm).
Change needle size if necessary to obtain the correct gauge.

Notions
Yarn needle, yarn bobbins (optional), thirty approximately ½" to 1" buttons, beads, or coins for backgammon pieces—15 each in two contrasting shapes or colors (shown with One World Button Supply Co. small filigree brass beads KUM-313 and small spiderweb brass beads KUM-306), four 1" buttons for attaching board to tote (shown with One World Button Supply Co. bleached horn button NPL 270-25XBL), one 1¼" button for tote closure (shown with One World Button Supply Co. bleached horn button NPL 270-34XBL), storebought dice and doubling cube.

Gauge
29 sts and 42 rows = 4" in cartridge belt rib pattern for tote.
21 sts and 28 rows = 4" in Stockinette stitch (St st) for board.

notes

- The checkerboard is worked using a double-knitting technique that creates a double-faced (reversible) fabric. The only difference between the two sides is that the colors are reversed: a square that is the color sand on one side is the color sea on the reverse side. It is important to use a circular needle so you can slide the work to the opposite end of the needle when required.

- Sl (slip) stitches as if to purl with yarn in front, unless otherwise specified.

- **Ssk (slip, slip, knit):** Slip the next 2 sts to right-hand needle one at a time as if to knit, pass them back to left-hand needle one at a time in their new orientation, and knit them together through the back of their loops.

- **K1tbl:** Knit one stitch through the back of its loop, twisting it.

- **K1f&b:** Knit into front and back of same stitch to increase one stitch.

- **Cartridge Belt Rib (multiple of 4 stitches, plus 3)**
  ROW 1: K3, *sl 1, k3; repeat from * to end.
  ROW 2: K1, *sl 1, k3; repeat from * to last 2 sts, end sl 1, k1.
  Repeat these 2 rows for pattern.

- **Half Double Crochet (hdc):** Yarn over hook, insert hook in st, draw up a loop, yarn over hook, draw through all 3 loops on hook.

- **Crochet Slip Stitch (sl st):** Insert hook in st, yarn over hook, and draw through loop on hook.

BACKGAMMON BOARD CHART

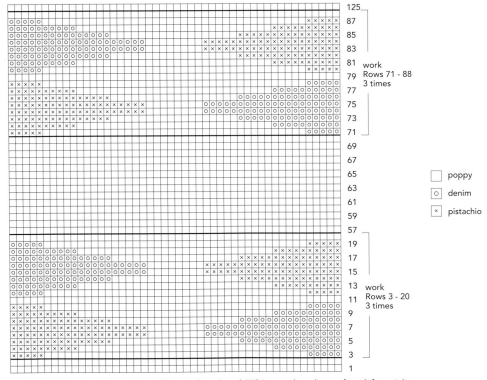

Work RS (odd-numbered) rows from right to left, and work WS (un-numbered) rows from left to right.

BOTTOM, SIDES, AND STRAP
(worked in one piece)

Using pistachio, CO 23 sts. Work in cartridge belt rib until piece measures 69" or desired length. BO all sts.

FINISHING

Sew CO and BO ends of strap together. Centering the strap seam on the bottom of the tote, sew front and back to strap along bottom and sides of front and back, leaving the last 4½" of back free for flap closure (the end with the buttonhole). Sew one 1¼" button to center front of tote, 2" down from top edge of front. Sew two 1" buttons to front, positioned 3½" down from top edge, and 1½" in from each side edge. Sew two 1" buttons to back, positioned 9" down from buttonhole edge of flap, and 1½" in from each side edge

Backgammon Board

The board is worked in St st, using separate yarn butterflies or yarn bobbins for the different-colored points, and carrying the background color behind from edge to edge. Secure the floats of the background color behind the points by twisting the colors around each other every 2 – 3 sts. Using poppy, CO 54 sts and work 6 rows garter stitch (knit all sts every row). Keeping 3 sts in garter stitch at each side, work backgammon board chart over center 48 sts. Work Rows 1 and 2 once, repeat Rows 3 – 20 three times (56 rows completed), work Rows 57 – 70 once, repeat Rows 71 – 88 three times (124 rows completed), work Row 125 once. Discontinue denim and pistachio, and work 6 rows garter stitch with poppy. BO all sts. Block lightly, if desired.

Ties (make 4): Using poppy, CO 2 sts and knit until piece measures 10". BO all sts. Attach the center of a tie to each corner of the board, and tie to 1" tote buttons as shown in photograph, wrapping board around the bottom of the tote.

Checkers Tote

With sea, CO 10 sts and arrange 2 sts each on five dpn, and use sixth dpn for working sts. Pm (place marker) for beginning of rnd (round).

(RND) 1: Knit each st through the back of loop, twisting it.

RNDS 2 AND 3: Knit all sts.

RND 4: K1f&b (see Notes) in the st at each end of all five needles—20 sts.

RNDS 5 AND 6: Knit all sts.

RND 7: K1f&b in the st at each end of all five needles—30 sts

RND 8: Knit all sts.

Work in rnds as follows, changing colors as indicated, and changing to circ needle when there are too many sts to fit comfortably on the dpns.

Change to sand and work Rnds 4–8 once—50 sts.
Change to merlot and work Rnds 4–8 once—70 sts.
Change to wintergreen and work Rnds 4–8 once—90 sts.
Change to sand and work Rnds 4–8 once—110 sts.
Change to sea and work Rnds 4–8 once—130 sts.
Change to sand and work Rnds 4–8 once—150 sts.
Change to merlot and work Rnds 4–8 once—170 sts.
Change to wintergreen and work Rnds 4–8 once—190 sts.

Work even on 190 sts in stripe pattern as follows:
    4 rnds sand.
    8 rnds *each* sea, sand, wintergreen, and merlot.
    4 rnds sand, increasing 2 sts on last rnd—192 sts.

Work in stranded colorwork St st as follows, carrying color not in use loosely across WS of work:

RNDS 1–4: *K4 sea, k4 wintergreen; repeat from * around.

RNDS 5–8: *K4 merlot, k4 sea; repeat from * around.

DRAWSTRING CASING

Change to wintergreen and work back and forth in St st on the first 96 sts for 20 rows. BO all sts. Rejoin wintergreen and repeat for remaining 96 sts. Fold casing sections in half and sew BO edges to beginning of wintergreen stripe on inside of bag, leaving openings between the sections for drawstring.

DRAWSTRING

Cut three strands of merlot approximately three times the length of the desired drawstring (the bag pictured uses 180" strands). With strands held together, fold them in half and place the looped end over a doorknob. Separately twist each group of three strands clockwise very tightly until they begin to kink. Keeping the strands taut, carefully allow the two groups to twist back onto each other, guiding the twist evenly into the finished drawstring. Remove from doorknob. Tie an overhand knot at each end of the drawstring, and trim the ends. Thread drawstring through casing as shown, and tie ends together.

CHECKERS

Finished Measurements
Large Striped Bag: 14" high and 19" wide.
Board: 12" square.
Game Pieces Bag: 6" high and 5" wide.

Yarn
Mission Falls 1824 Cotton (100% cotton; 84 yards / 50 grams): #104 sand, 4 skeins; #402 sea (blue), #208 merlot (wine red), and #302 wintergreen (green), 3 skeins each.

Needles
One 29" circular (circ) needle size US 6 (4 mm). Six double-pointed needles (dpn) size US 6 (4 mm). Change needle size if necessary to obtain the correct gauge.

Notions
Yarn needle, stitch marker or coilless safety pin, crochet hook size H/8 (5 mm), 12 light and 12 dark approximately ½" to 1" buttons, beads, or coins for checkers (shown with One World Button Supply Co. recycled glass beads T-09 Amber and T-09 Dark Blue).

Gauge
20 sts and 32 rounds = 4" in Stockinette stitch (St st) for checkers bags.
18 sts (three 6-stitch squares) = 4¼" wide and 24 rows (three 8-row squares) = 4" high, in double-knitting for checkerboard.

Checkerboard

With sea and circ needle, CO 42 sts. Next row: K1, k1f&b in each of the next 40 sts, k1—82 sts.

ROW 1: With sea, k1, *[yb (bring yarn to back of work), k1, yf (bring yarn to front of work), sl (slip) 1] 5 times, [yb, sl 1, yf, p1] 5 times; repeat from * 3 more times, k1. Slide work to opposite end of needle, ready to work another row starting at the same side as Row 1.

ROW 2: With sand, K1, *[yb, sl 1, yf, p1] 5 times, [yb, k1, yf, sl 1] 5 times; repeat from * 3 more times, k1, turn.

ROW 3: With sand, k1, *[yb, sl 1, yf, p1] 5 times, [yb, k1, yf, sl 1] 5 times; repeat from * 3 more times, k1, slide work to opposite end of needle, ready to work another row starting at the same side.

ROW 4: With sea, k1, *[yb, k1, yf, sl 1] 5 times, [yb, sl 1, yf, p1] 5 times; repeat from * 3 more times, k1, turn.

ROW 5: With sea, k1, *[yb, k1, yf, sl 1] 5 times, [yb, sl 1, yf, p1] 5 times; repeat from * 3 more times, k1, slide.

ROWS 6-13: Repeat Rows 2–5 twice.

ROWS 14-16: Repeat Rows 2–4. One row of checkerboard squares has been completed.

ROW 17: With sand, k1 *[yb, k1, yf, sl 1] 5 times, [yb, sl 1, yf, p1] 5 times; repeat from * 3 more times, k1, slide.

ROW 18: With sea, k1 *[yb, sl 1, yf, p1] 5 times, [yb, k1, yf, sl 1] 5 times; repeat from * 3 more times, k1, turn.

ROW 19: With sea, k1 *[yb, sl 1, yf, p1] 5 times, [yb, k1, yf, sl 1] 5 times; repeat from * 3 more times, k1, slide.

ROW 20: With sand, k1 *[yb, k1, yf, sl 1] 5 times, [yb, sl 1, yf, p1] 5 times; repeat from * 3 more times, k1, turn.

ROWS 21-28: Repeat Rows 17–20 twice.

ROWS 29-32: Repeat Rows 17–20.

The second row of checkerboard squares has been completed. Repeat Rows 1–32 three more times for an 8 x 8 checkerboard grid. Break off sea. With sand, work 1 row on all sts as foll: k1, *k1, p1; repeat from * to last st, end k1. Next row: k1, ssk (see Notes) across to last st, end k1—42 sts. BO all sts.

FINISHING

Using crochet hook and wintergreen, attach yarn at one corner and draw up a loop. Work 2 hdc (see Notes) in corner stitch, then work 1 hdc in each st around, working 3 hdc into each of the next 3 corner sts. End with 1 hdc in the corner where you began. Join first and last sts using a crochet sl st (see Notes). Fasten off.

Checkers Game Pieces Bag

With sand, CO 8 sts and arrange 2 sts each on four dpn. Place a stitch marker or coilless safety pin in the work to indicate beginning of rnd.

RND 1: Knit each st through the back of its loop, twisting it.

RNDS 2, 4, 6, 8, AND 10: Knit all sts.

RND 3: K1f&b (see Notes) in the st at each end of all four needles—16 sts.

RND 5: Repeat Rnd 3—24 sts.

RND 7: Repeat Rnd 3—32 sts.

RND 9: Repeat Rnd 3—40 sts

RND 11: Repeat Rnd 3—48 sts.

RND 12: Knit all sts.

Work even in St st until piece measures 4" from CO. Work next 6 rnds in stripes as follows: 2 rnds merlot, 2 rnds sand, 2 rnds merlot. Change to sand and knit 1 rnd.

DRAWSTRING CASING

Work back and forth on the first 24 sts for 12 rows. BO all sts. Rejoin sand and repeat for remaining 24 sts. Fold casing sections in half and sew BO edges to beginning of last sand stripe on inside of bag, leaving openings between the sections for drawstring.

DRAWSTRING

Using two 60" strands of merlot, make drawstring same as for checkers large striped bag using 2 instead of 3 strands for each section. Thread drawstring through casing as shown and tie ends together.

body and soul 1

lopi lace scarf

PAM ALLEN

The femininity of lace and the ruggedness of Lopi yarn from Iceland are beautifully merged in this casual scarf. It is shown in three colorways (here and on page 103) because designer Pam Allen and I just couldn't narrow down our choice to a single color when we looked at the broad and beautiful palette in which this classic yarn is offered. The scarf's simple lace pattern forms gentle waves along all four edges.

notes

- **Yo (yarnover):** Bring yarn to the front and over the right-hand needle. Work the newly-created loop as a st on the next row.

- **Ssk (slip, slip, knit):** Slip the next 2 sts to right-hand needle one at a time as if to knit, pass them back to left-hand needle one at a time in their new orientation, and knit them together through the back of their loops.

Finished Measurements
8" wide by 52" long, after blocking.

Yarn
Reynolds Lite-Lopi (100% Icelandic wool; 109 yards / 50 grams): 2 skeins main color (MC) and 1 skein optional contrast color (CC). Scarf shown in #428 rose heather (MC) with #421 celery heather (CC), #421 celery heather (MC) with #418 light blue heather (CC), and #418 light blue heather (MC) with #428 rose heather (CC).

Needles
One set straight needles size US 10 (6 mm). One set straight needles size US 10½ (6.5 mm). One set straight needles size US 11 (8 mm). Change needle size if necessary to obtain the correct gauge.

Notions
Yarn needle.

Gauge
Using size 10 needles, 14½ sts and 19 rows = 4" in lace pattern, after blocking.

Using size 11 needles and MC, or CC for contrasting edge, CO 29 sts.

ROW 1: (RS) Change to size 10½ needles, k2, *p1, k1; rep from * to last 3 sts, end p1, k2.

ROW 2: Purl.

ROW 3: Change to size 10 needles and MC, if you are not already using it. K2, *(p1, k1) 3 times, (yo, k2tog) twice (see Notes); rep from * once more, (p1, k1) twice, p1, k2.

ROW 4: Purl.

ROWS 5 – 12: Rep Rows 3 and 4 four times.

ROW 13: (RS) K2, p1, *(ssk, yo) twice (see Notes), (k1, p1) 3 times; rep from * once more, (ssk, yo) twice, k2.

ROW 14: Purl.

ROWS 15 – 22: Repeat Rows 13 and 14 four times.

Repeat Rows 3 – 22 until piece measures approximately 48" relaxed, ending with Row 12. For a contrasting edge, break off MC and change to CC. Change to size 10½ needles, work Rows 1 and 2 of pattern. Using size 11 needles, BO in rib.

Block to finished measurements.

and neck warmer

WENDY EASTON

A lot of serious knitters believed it couldn't be done—that is, brioche stitch in the round. In fact, when I called my friend Therese Inverso to tell her about the Brioche Hat (pages 65, 66, and 74) and Neck Warmer (page 66), both of which are knitted in the round, she was very suspicious. "Even the great Elizabeth (knitting icon and in-the-round devotee Elizabeth Zimmermann [1910–1999]) didn't do brioche in the round," she said. But it was Elizabeth's daughter, Meg Swansen, who had introduced me to this project's designer, Wendy Easton, impressed as she was with Wendy's unique and imaginative approach to knitting. Although they never met, Wendy considers Elizabeth a mentor, and for this project she presents three techniques based on Elizabeth's innovations: the two-strand tubular cast-on, the built-in I-cord edging, and the tubular bind-off.

Review notes on page 64 before beginning to knit.

Scarf

Using larger needles and provisional cast-on (see Notes) or other temporary cast-on of your choice, CO 3 sts and make a 2-color I-cord as follows: Knit 3 with L, slide sts to the end of needle where you started, join D, *k3 with D, slide sts to the end of needle where you started, k3 with L, slide sts to end of needle where you started; rep from * until you have completed 29 rows total, ending with a row of L. Do not cut yarns. Change

Finished Measurements
Scarf: 7" wide x 54" long.
Hat: Approximately 21" around.
Neck Warmer: Approximately 21" around x 8" high.

Yarn
Brown Sheep Lamb's Pride Worsted (85% wool, 15% mohair; 190 yards / 4 ounces): 1 skein each of dark (D) and light (L) colors for *each* piece; 3 skeins each of D and L for the entire set. Shown in #M89 roasted coffee with #M23 fuchsia, #M47 Tahiti teal with #M69 old sage, and #M42 twilight green with #M69 old sage.

Needles
Scarf: Two double-pointed needles (dpn) size US 8 (5 mm). Two dpn size US 10½ (6.5 mm).
Hat: One 16" circular (circ) needle size US 6 (4 mm). One 16" circ needle size US 8 (5 mm). One set of five dpn size US 8 (5 mm); you may use the circ. needle as your fifth needle if you only have a set of four dpn.
Neck Warmer: One 16" circ or set of four dpn size US 8 (5 mm).
Change needle size if necessary to obtain the correct gauge.

Notions
Yarn needle, stitch marker, 2 yards thin smooth scrap yarn for provisional cast-on (optional).

Gauge
14 sts and 40 rows/rnds = 4" in bicolor brioche pattern. Each st in the dominant column of slip sts can be counted as 2 rows/rnds.

Brioche Scarf in Tahiti teal and old sage.

notes

- All stitches are sl (slipped) as if to purl with yarn in front unless otherwise specified.

- **Yo (yarnover):** Bring yarn to the front and over the right-hand needle. Work the newly-created loop as a st on the next row.

- **Sl 1 Yo followed by a Knit St:** Bring yarn to front of work, sl 1 as if to purl, bring the yarn over the needle to the back, and knit the next st, forming the yo automatically as you do so.

- **Sl 1 Yo followed by a Purl St:** With yarn in front, sl 1, bring yarn over needle and to front, ready to purl.

- When changing colors in bicolor brioche stitch, drop the old color and start the new color by bringing it up from under the old color. Do not twist the yarns around each other at the color changes.

- **Provisional Cast-On:** Using a thin, smooth scrap yarn, CO the required number of sts and work in Stockinette st (St st) for 3 – 4 rows. Change to main yarn and continue as directed.

- **Kitchener Stitch:** On a yarn needle, thread a length of yarn approximately 4 times the length of the section to be joined. Hold needles with sts to be grafted with purl sides of work together. Working from right to left, *insert yarn needle in first stitch on front needle as if to knit, pull yarn through, remove st from needle. Insert yarn needle into next st on front needle as if to purl, pull yarn through, leave st on needle. Insert yarn needle into first st on back needle as if to purl, pull yarn through, remove st from needle. Insert yarn needle into next st on back needle as if to knit, pull yarn through, leave st on needle. Repeat from * until 1 st remains on each needle. Cut yarn and pass through last 2 sts to fasten off.

- **Two-Strand Tubular Cast-On:** Knot the two yarns together (later you will remove this knot and weave in the ends). Hold this knotted end in your right hand, gripping the two yarns in your left hand the same as you would for a long-tail cast-on, with the D yarn up and over your index finger and the L yarn down and around your thumb "slingshot" fashion. Now, with the right-hand needle (holding the knot snugly against this needle) direct the point of the right-hand needle down, under, and up behind the L strand to reach up and catch the D strand, which you will bring up from under the L. Now you have one D st on the needle. Next, direct the point of the right-hand needle over and behind the D strand on your index finger, catch the L strand and bring it up from under the D one. Your second st on the needle is this L one. Continue until you have the required number of sts. Join for working in the rnd (round), being careful not to twist, and pm (place marker) to indicate the beginning of the rnd. If any CO sts appear twisted or incorrectly mounted, correct them as you work the set-up rnd.

- **Tubular Bind-Off:** Trim yarn to about 4 times the length of edge to be BO, and thread on a yarn needle. As you work, do not pull the yarn too tightly; try to match the tension of the rest of the knitting. *Insert yarn needle into St 1 on the left-hand needle as if to knit and remove it from the needle. Insert yarn needle as if to purl in front of work into St 3 (now the 2nd st remaining on the left-hand needle, a knit st) and pull yarn through. Insert yarn needle as if to purl into St 2 (now the 1st st remaining on the left-hand needle) and remove it from the needle. Working around the back of St 3 (now the first st on left-hand needle), insert the yarn needle into St 4 (now the 2nd st on left-hand needle) as if to knit and pull the yarn through. Repeat from * until you have BO all sts. Fasten off last st. Cut yarn and pass through the last st to fasten off.

to smaller dpn. Sl (slip) the 3 L sts just worked to a dpn, then skipping the D row closest to the needle, pick up and knit (using L) one side of the edge st in each of the next 25 I-cord rows on dpn, skip the final D row, carefully remove the provisional cast-on yarn and pick up 3 L sts from the base of the first L row of I-cord—31 sts on needle. Cut L. Slide sts to end of needle where you started, ready to work a row with D on smaller needles.

SET-UP ROW: With D, knit 3 I-cord sts, sl 1, yo (see Notes), *k1, sl 1, yo; repeat from * until 3 I-cord sts remain at end of row, sl these last 3 sts as if to purl with yarn in front (see Notes). Slide sts to end of needle where you started, ready to work a row with L—44 sts on needle: 3 I-cord sts at each side, 38 brioche pattern sts (including yarnovers).

ROW 1: Join L, k3, p2tog (the sl st and its yo), *sl 1, yo, p2tog; repeat from * to last 3 sts, sl last 3 sts—43 sts. Turn work.

ROW 2: With D, k3, sl 1, yo, *p2tog (the sl st and its yo), sl 1, yo; repeat from * to last 3 sts, sl last 3 sts as before—44 sts. Slide sts to end of needle where you started, ready to work a row with L.

ROW 3: With L, k3, k2tog (the sl st and its yo), *sl 1, yo, k2tog; repeat from * to last 3 sts, sl last 3 sts as before—43 sts. Turn work.

ROW 4: With D, k3, sl 1, yo, *k2tog (the sl st and its yo), sl 1, yo; repeat from * to last 3 sts, sl last 3 sts as before—44 sts. Slide sts to end of needle where you started, ready to work a row with L.

Repeat Rows 1–4 (do not repeat the set-up row) until piece measures 54" or desired length,

ending with Row 1 (both yarns at the same side of the work). Change to larger needles. To turn the corner, knit the first 3 sts with D, then slide sts to end of needle where you started, ready to work a row with L. Work top border as follows: Using L first, *k2, sl 1, k1 from the live sts on smaller needle, psso (pass slipped st over), slide sts to end of needle where you started, change to D k2, sl 1, k2tog (the sl st and its yo), psso, slide sts to end of needle where you

started; rep from *, alternating colors each row as for bottom border, until 6 sts remain (3 I-cord sts each from the top and side borders). If the sts remaining are all the same color, arrange them on two needles with wrong sides held together, and use the other color to graft the sts together using Kitchener stitch (see Notes). If there are 3 sts of each color remaining, work 1 more row on the first 3 sts so all 6 sts are the same color. Arrange and graft as above. Weave in ends.

Brioche Hat in Tahiti teal and old sage.

Hat

With smaller circ needle, CO 64 sts using two-strand tubular cast-on (see Notes).

SET-UP RND (ROUND): With D, *k1, sl 1, yo (see Notes); repeat from * to end, letting D yarn hang over right-hand needle to the back of work at the end of the rnd so as not to lose the final yo—96 sts (including the yarnovers).

RND 1: With L, *sl 1, yo, p2tog (the sl st and its yo); repeat from * to end.

RND 2: With D, *k2tog (the sl st and its yo), sl 1, yo; repeat from * to end, taking care not to lose the final yo at end of rnd.

Repeat Rnds 1 and 2 (do not repeat the set-up rnd) until piece measures 3". Change to larger circ needle and work in pattern as established until piece measures 9", ending with Rnd 1—96 sts on needles (including the yarnovers). Rearrange sts so there are 24 sts each on four dpn.

CROWN RND 1: With D, *[k2tog, sl 1, yo] twice, k2tog, k3tog (the next sl st, yo, and following st), sl 1, yo, sl next st and yo together as if to k2tog yb (with yarn in back), sl next st as if to knit yb, return 3 slipped sts to left-hand needle in their new orientation and k3tog tbl (through back of their loops), [k2tog, sl 1, yo] three times; repeat from * on each of next 3 needles.

CROWN RND 2: With L, continue in brioche stitch as established (Rnd 1 of brioche pattern), but when you come to 2 D sts next to each other, work them as follows: sl 1 as if to purl yf (with yarn in front), yo, sl 1 as if to purl with yb (making only 1 yo for this pair of sts).

Brioche Hat and Neck Warmer in roasted coffee and fuchsia.

CROWN RND 3: With D, continue in brioche stitch as established (Rnd 2 of brioche pattern), but when you come to 2 D sts next to each other, work them as k2tog (first D st and its yo), k1.

CROWN RND 4: Repeat Crown Rnd 2.

CROWN RND 5: With D, *[k2tog, sl 1, yo] twice, k3tog (the next sl st, yo, and following st), sl 1, yo, drop yo from left needle and let it fall behind the work, sl first D st as if to knit yb, sl the second D st as if to knit yb, pick up dropped yo loop and place on right-hand needle, return these last 3 sts to left-hand needle in their new orientation and k3tog tbl, [sl 1, yo, k2tog] twice, sl 1, yo; repeat from * on each of next 3 needles.

CROWN RND 6: With L, continue in brioche stitch as established.

CROWN RND 7: With D, continue in brioche stitch as established.

CROWN RND 8: With L, continue in brioche stitch as established.

CROWN RND 9: With D, *k2tog, sl 1, yo, k2tog, k3tog (the next sl st, yo, and following st), sl 1, yo, sl next st and yo as if to k2tog yb, sl next st as if to knit yb, pass 3 slipped sts back to left needle in their new orientation and k3tog tbl, [k2tog, sl 1, yo] twice; repeat from * on each of next 3 needles.

CROWN RND 10: Repeat Crown Rnd 2.

CROWN RND 11: Repeat Crown Rnd 3.

CROWN RND 12: Repeat Crown Rnd 2.

CROWN RND 13: With D, *k2tog, sl 1, yo, k3tog (the next sl st, yo, and following st), sl 1, yo, drop yo from left-hand needle and let it hang behind the work, sl first D st as if to knit yb, sl the second D st as if to knit yb, pick up dropped yo loop and place on right-hand needle, return

these last 3 sts to left-hand needle and k3tog tbl, sl 1, yo, k2tog, sl 1, yo; repeat from * on each of next 3 needles.

CROWN RND 14: With L, continue in brioche stitch as established.

CROWN RND 15: With D, continue in brioche stitch as established.

CROWN RND 16: With L, continue in brioche stitch as established.

CROWN RND 17: With D, *k2tog, k3tog (the next sl st, yo, and following st), sl 1, yo, sl next st and yo as if to k2tog yb, sl next st as if to knit yb, return 3 slipped sts to left-hand needle in their new orientation and k3tog tbl, k2tog, sl 1, yo; repeat from * on each of next 3 needles.

CROWN RND 18: With L, *sl 1 as if to purl yf, yo, sl 1 as if to purl with yb, p2tog; repeat from * to end.

CROWN RND 19: With D, *k3tog (the next sl st, yo, and following st), sl 1, yo, drop yo from left-hand needle and let it hang behind the work, sl first D st as if to knit yb, sl the second D st as if to knit yb, pick up dropped yo loop and place on right-hand needle, return these last 3 sts to left-hand needle in their new orientation and k3tog tbl, sl 1, yo; repeat from * to end.

CROWN RND 20: With L, *sl 1 as if to purl yb, p2tog; repeat from * to end.

CROWN RND 21: With D, *sl 2 sts one at a time as if to knit, return 2

slipped sts to left-hand needle in their new orientation, K2tog tbl; repeat from * to end—8 sts remain.

Break yarn, and with a yarn needle, draw the D yarn through the remaining 8 sts and secure on inside of hat. Untie the knot at the beginning of the CO and weave in ends. Fold up the bottom 3" of the hat to form a cuffed brim.

Neck Warmer

With circ needle or dpn, CO 64 sts using two-strand tubular cast-on method (see Notes). Cut the L cast-on strand, leaving an 8" tail to be woven in later, and work next 4 rnds with the remaining strand of D.

Work one row of k1, p1 ribbing as follows: *k1, p1; repeat from * to end.

SET-UP RND: *K1, sl 1, yo (see Notes); repeat from * to end.

RND 1: *Sl 1, yo, p2tog; repeat from * to end.

RND 2: *K2tog, sl 1, yo; repeat from * to end.

Join L yarn and work Rnd 1 with L, then work Rnd 2 with D (do not repeat the set-up rnd). Continue in pattern as established, alternating colors each rnd, so Rnd 1 will always be worked with L, and Rnd 2 will always be worked with D. Work until piece measures about 8", ending with Rnd 2. Cut D yarn. Work next 3 rnds of brioche pattern in L to correspond to the rnds of D at the beginning. Work 1 row k1, p1 ribbing in L as follows: *k1, p1; repeat from * to end.

BO using tubular bind-off (see Notes). Untie knot at beginning of tubular cast-on and weave in ends.

Imagination is

more important than

knowledge.

ALBERT EINSTEIN

cashmere pullover

TEVA DURHAM

Knocking around in a cashmere sweater is like drinking hot chocolate made with the finest bittersweet chocolate. It's warm and soothing and kind of decadent. Knit the sweater yourself, and the experience lasts even longer and is even more pleasurable.

Teva Durham's goal in designing this unisex pullover was to create something at once modern and ancient, a bit like a rugby shirt, a bit like a monastic tunic, rough-hewn yet soft and luxurious. The cashmere tweed yarn with its organic (pebble, sandstone) look adds to the textural contrast and, Teva raves, "is absolutely delicious to knit with."

Unusual for a handknit, this garment is reversible: one side is Reverse Stockinette stitch with Stockinette accents (page 72) and exposed seaming, and the other side is Stockinette stitch with Reverse Stockinette-stitch accents (at right). Once the two center body pieces have been completed, the lower body sections are worked by picking up stitches and knitting downward. The front sleeve/yoke section is worked by picking up stitches from the center front section and working to the shoulders where the neck opening and collar are completed. The back sleeve/yoke section is worked from the shoulders down to the center back section. Finishing is minimal—just the sleeve and side seams when the knitting is done.

Finished Measurements
36 (40, 44, 48)" chest. Sweater shown measures 40".

Yarn
Classic Elite Indulge (100% cashmere; 55 yards / 50 grams): (9, 10, 12, 14) skeins. Shown in #60051 natural (tan/gray mix).

Needles
One 32" circular (circ) needle size US 10½ (6.5 mm).
One 16" circ needle size US 10½ (6.5 mm).
Change needle size if necessary to obtain the correct gauge.

Notions
Stitch markers, yarn needle.

Gauge
12 sts and 16 rows = 4" in Stockinette stitch (St st).

Review notes on page 70 before beginning to knit.

CENTER BODY SECTION
(worked side-to-side; make 2)
With either length circ needle, loosely cast on 29 sts using long-tail cast-on (see Notes).
ROW 1: Sl (slip) 1 (selvage st; see Notes), purl to end.
ROW 2: Sl 1 (selvage st; see Notes), knit to end. These 2 rows form the Rev St st border.
ROW 3: Sl 1, knit to end.
ROW 4: Sl 1, purl to end.

notes

- Although there are technically no RS or WS rows, most shaping is done when Reverse Stockinette (Rev St st) side is facing.

- **Selvage Stitches:** Most pieces have a slip st selvedge at the beginning of each row given in the instructions. Unless otherwise specified, if the st after the slip st is a purl, slip as if to purl yf (with yarn in front); and if the st after the slip st is a knit, slip as if to knit yb (with yarn in back).

- Because the garment is reversible it is best to weave in the ends by separating the yarn's 3 plies and running them through purl heads of the stitches; individual plies are less obtrusive and less likely to work their way loose.

- **Long-tail Cast-On** (also known as **Continental Cast-on**): Leaving a tail with about 1" of yarn for each st to be cast-on, make a slipknot in the yarn and place it on the right-hand needle. Insert the thumb and forefinger of your left hand between the strands of yarn so the working end is around your forefinger, and the tail end is around your thumb "slingshot" fashion. Insert the tip of the right-hand needle into the loop on the thumb, hook the strand of yarn coming from the forefinger, and draw up a loop with the right-hand needle. Remove your thumb from the loop and pull on the working yarn to tighten the new stitch on the right-hand needle. Return your thumb and forefinger to their original positions, and repeat until you have cast on the number of stitches required.

- **M1 (make 1):** Increase on Rev St st side as follows: Insert tip of left-hand needle under the strand between the two needles, from front to back, and lift this strand onto the left-hand needle. Purl the lifted strand through the back of loop, twisting it to avoid making a hole.

- **Ssk (slip, slip, knit):** Slip the next 2 sts to right-hand needle one at a time as if to knit, pass them back to left-hand needle one at a time in their new orientation and knit them together through the back of their loops.

- **Kitchener Stitch:** On a yarn needle, thread a length of yarn approximately 4 times the length of the section to be joined. Hold needles with sts to be grafted with purl sides of work together. Working from right to left, *insert yarn needle in first stitch on front needle as if to knit, pull yarn through, remove st from needle. Insert yarn needle into next st on front needle as if to purl, pull yarn through, leave st on needle. Insert yarn needle into first st on back needle as if to purl, pull yarn through, remove st from needle. Insert yarn needle into next st on back needle as if to knit, pull yarn through, leave st on needle. Repeat from * until 1 st remains on each needle. Cut yarn and pass through the last 2 sts to fastion off.

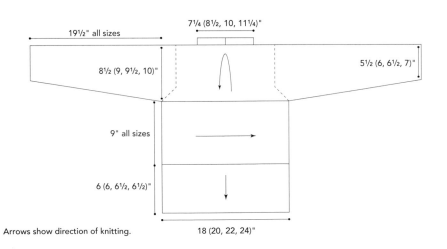

7¼ (8½, 10, 11¼)"

19½" all sizes

8½ (9, 9½, 10)"

5½ (6, 6½, 7)"

9" all sizes

6 (6, 6½, 6½)"

18 (20, 22, 24)"

Arrows show direction of knitting.

Repeat Rows 3 and 4 (St st) until piece measures 17¼ (19¼, 21¼, 23¼)". Work Rows 1 and 2 once for second Rev St st border. BO all sts loosely in Rev St st. Total length of piece measures 18 (20, 22, 24)".

FRONT YOKE AND SLEEVES
(make 1)

Hold center body section with the Rev St st side facing you, and one long selvage edge uppermost. Using longer circ needle, and peering over the top edge to look at the other side of the fabric, and *allowing the slipped selvage sts to roll to the side of work facing you, insert left needle tip from left to right into the left side of the st just inside the first selvedge st, and knit the picked up st. Repeat from * across, picking up a total of 54 (60, 66, 72) sts evenly along the selvage edge of center body section (approximately 3 sts picked up for every 4 rows).

ROW 1: (St st side) CO 10 sts onto left-hand needle and knit them, pm (place marker), p1 ("seam" stitch), knit to last st, p1 ("seam" stitch)—64 (70, 76, 82) sts.

ROW 2: (Rev St st side) CO 10 sts as before and purl them, M1 (see Notes), pm, ssk (see Notes), purl to 2 sts before marker, k2tog, slip marker, M1, purl to end—74 (80, 86, 92) sts.

ROW 3: (St st side) CO 10 sts and knit them, knit to marker, slip marker, sl 1 as if to purl yf, knit to 1 st before marker, sl 1 as if to purl yf, slip marker, knit to end—84 (90, 96, 102) sts.

ROW 4: (Rev St st side) CO 10 sts and purl them, purl to marker, slip marker off needle, M1, replace marker, ssk, purl to 2 sts before marker, k2tog, slip marker, M1, purl to end—(94, 100, 106, 112) sts.

Continue in this manner for 8 more rows, increasing 1 st outside of markers and decreasing 1 st inside of markers every Rev St st side row, slipping the "seam" sts every St st side row, *and at the same time,* continue to CO 10 sts at beg of next 4 rows, then CO 9 sts at beg of following 4 rows, ending with a Rev St st side row—170 (176, 182, 188) sts.

ROW 1: (St st side) Sl 1 (selvage st), p2, knit to marker, slip marker, sl 1 as if to purl yf, knit to 1 st before marker, sl 1 as if to purl yf, slip marker, knit to last 3 sts, end p3.

ROW 2: (Rev St st side) Sl 1 (selvage st), k2, purl to marker, slip marker off needle, M1, replace marker, ssk, purl to 2 sts before marker, k2tog, slip marker, M1, purl to last 3 sts, end k3.

Repeat last 2 rows once—170 (176, 182, 188) sts, 38 (44, 50, 56) sts between markers, 66 sts total at each side for sleeves, with 3 of the sleeve sts at each end of needle worked in the opposite stitch pattern from the dominant pattern to form the cuffs. Work even in patterns as established (with no further increases or decreases), slipping selvage sts as before, knitting "seam" sts on Rev St st side rows, and slipping "seam" sts as before on St st side rows, until piece measures 8¼ (8¾, 9¼, 9¾)" from pickup row, ending with a St st side row.

COLLAR

On next Rev St st row, work to "seam" st, sl 1 as if to purl yb, k7 (8, 9, 10), with shorter circ needle knit center 22 (26, 30, 34) sts, then CO another 22 (26, 30, 34) sts onto shorter circ needle—44 (52, 60, 68) sts on shorter needle, 74 (75, 76, 77) sts just worked on longer needle, 74 (75, 76, 77) sts

remaining unworked on longer needle. Secure the sts on the longer circ needle and let that needle hang out of the way temporarily. Working on shorter needle sts only, join sts into a circle, being careful not to twist, p8 (10, 12, 14), k2 (you will be at center front neck), pm for end of row, turn, and work neckband back and forth in rows on shorter needle as follows:

ROW 1: (St st side) Sl 1 (selvage st), p1, knit to last 2 sts, end p2.

ROW 2: (Rev St st side) Sl 1 (selvage st), k1, purl to last 2 sts, end k2.

Repeat the last 2 rows once , then purl 1 row on St st side. BO loosely as if to knit on Rev St st side.

BACK YOKE AND SLEEVES

With Rev St st side facing, join yarn to beginning of sts left unworked on longer needle, k7 (8, 9, 10), sl 1 (selvage st), purl to last 3 sts, k3. Next row (St st side): Sl 1 as if to purl yf, p2, knit to "seam" st, sl 1 as if to purl yf, p7 (8, 9, 10), pick up and knit 22 (26, 30, 34) sts along CO edge of collar, p7 (8, 9, 10), sl 1 as if to purl yf, knit to last 3 sts, p3—170 (176, 182, 188) sts. Next row (Rev St st side): Sl 1 (selvage st), k2, purl to "seam" st, k1, purl to other "seam" st, k1, purl to last 3 sts, k3. Work even in patterns as established, slipping selvage sts as before, knitting "seam" sts on Rev St st side rows, slipping "seam" sts on St st side rows, and maintaining patterns at cuffs, until piece measures 4½ (5, 5½, 6)" from sts picked up at base of collar, ending with a St st side row. Begin traveling "seam" st to match front as foll:

ROW 1: (Rev St st side) Work as established until 1 st before "seam" st, k2tog, pm, M1, work to next "seam" st, M1, place marker, ssk, work as established to end.

ROW 2: (St st side) Work as established to 1 st before marker, sl 1 as if to purl yf, knit to next marker, sl 1 as if to purl yf, work to end.

Repeat Rows 1 and 2 once more—piece measures 5½ (6, 6½, 7)" from base of collar. Repeat Rows 1 and 2 three more times, then continue as established and *at the same time*, BO 9 sts at beg of next 4 rows, then BO 10 sts at beg of following 8 rows, ending with a St st side row—54 (60, 66, 72) sts remain, with "seam" st at each end of needle. Set longer circ needle with live sts aside temporarily.

Hold remaining center body section with the Rev St st side facing you, and one long selvage edge uppermost. Allowing the slipped selvage sts to roll to the side of work facing you, inserting needle tip from back to front, pick up the left side loops of 54 (60, 66, 72) sts evenly along the selvage edge of center body section (approximately 3 sts picked up for every 4 rows), using the same needle holding the yoke sts. Fold needle in half and hold garment pieces together with St st sides touching and Rev St st sides facing outward. Using the shorter circ needle, BO the two sections together as follows: Insert the needle tip into the first st on each end of the longer circ needle (one st each from center section and yoke) and knit these 2 sts together, *knit the next st of each section together in the same manner, pass the first st on right-hand needle over the second to BO; repeat from * until all sts have been joined. Cut yarn and draw through last st to fasten off.

SEW SEAMS

Sew sleeve and side seams as invisibly as possible, or graft edges together on St st side of work for a reversible seam as follows: Turn garment inside out so St st side is facing you. Using longer circ needle with St st facing, pick up and knit 1 st in the outer half of each edge st along one of the pieces to be seamed. Pick up sts along the edge of the other piece to be seamed. Use Kitchener stitch (see Notes) to graft the sts together.

LOWER BODY SECTION
(make 2)

Hold garment upside-down with selvage edge of center body section upper most and Rev St st side facing you. Beginning at side seam, and allowing slipped selvage sts to roll to the side of work facing you, pick up and knit 54 (60, 66, 72) sts evenly across lower back edge to other side seam, as picked up for yoke and sleeves (approximately 3 sts for every 4 rows). Next row: (St st side) Sl 1 (selvage st), p2, knit to last 3 sts, end p3. Next row: (Rev St st side) Sl 1 (selvage st), k2, purl to last 3 sts, end k3. Repeat the last 2 rows until piece measures 5¼ (5¼, 5¾, 5¾)" from pickup row. Purl across next St st side row, then knit across next Rev St st row. BO loosely as if to purl on St st side. Repeat for lower body section of front. Weave in ends. Block lightly to finished measurements.

ADRIENNE'S Hot Chocolate

Adrienne Welch is an old friend, a renowned chocolatier with her own chocolate company, Adrienne's Chocolates, and an excellent knitter with her own pattern company, Arachne Designs. When I spoke to her about a hot-chocolate recipe for this book, I thought she might think it was an odd idea. Instead, she laughed, and said knitting and chocolate are intimately intertwined for her and her knitting group in St. Louis. Here is the recipe she generously shared. It is thick, rich, and delicious—very much like the decadent hot chocolate traditionally served in France. This recipe yields one serving—to make more, simply multiply each quantity by the number of people you want to indulge.

1 tablespoon high-quality unsweetened cocoa powder, such as Valrhona or Hershey's European-style

½ teaspoon granulated sugar

Few grains of salt

⅔ cup 2-percent milk

¼ cup chopped, high-quality bittersweet chocolate, such as Valrhona, Callebaut, or Michelle Cuizel

Dash of cognac (optional)

In a small bowl, combine the cocoa powder, sugar, and salt. Set aside. In a small saucepan over medium-low heat, warm the milk until hot, but not boiling. Add about 1 tablespoon of the milk to the cocoa mixture, and stir to make a paste. Add the paste and the chopped chocolate to the saucepan of hot milk, place back over medium-low heat, and cook, stirring continuously with a whisk, until the chocolate melts and the mixture is hot, but not boiling. Whisk the mixture until frothy, then pour into a preheated mug. Add cognac, if desired.

berkshire pullover

MARGRIT LOHRER

Margrit Lohrer named this comfortable, quick-knit pullover after a beautiful region of New York and Massachusetts. The Berkshires are a very popular destination for weekend travelers looking for a mixture of idyllic scenery, arts and culture, fine dining, outdoor sports, and tranquility. A great place for a vacation chockful of knitting! Margrit compares the simplicity and comfort of this pullover to our favorite sweatshirts, the ones we want to own in every color and wear every weekend. This sweater is worked in one piece to the underarms, then the front and back are worked separately to the shoulders.

Finished Measurements
35 (38½, 41½, 45, 49)" chest. Sweater shown measures 41½".

Yarn
Morehouse Merino Bulky (100% Merino wool; 102 yards / 4 ounces): 6 (7, 8, 9, 10) skeins. Shown in oatmeal and hemlock.

Needles
One 24" or 29" circ (circular) needle size US 13 (9 mm).
One 16" circ needle size US 13 (9 mm) for neck finishing.
One set double-pointed needles (dpn) size US 13 (9 mm) for sleeves.
Change needle size if necessary to obtain correct gauge.

Notions
Stitch marker, stitch holders, yarn needle.

Gauge
10 sts and 18 rows = 4" in Stockinette stitch (St st).

BODY

With longer circ needle, CO 88 (96, 104, 112, 122) sts. Join for working in the rnd (round), being careful not to twist sts, and place marker to indicate beginning of rnd. Work in St st (Stockinette stitch) until piece measures 15 (16, 17, 18, 19)" from beginning. Divide for armholes as follows: Knit 44 (48, 52, 56, 61) sts for front, turn; purl to beginning of rnd. Remove marker; place remaining sts on holder for back. Work even in St st, back and forth on front sts, knitting the first and last sts on every row for selvages, until armhole measures 7½ (8, 8½, 9, 9½)", ending with a WS row. Measure out about 2½ yards of yarn (used later to BO the front and back together at shoulders); break yarn. Place sts on holder.

Return back sts to needle; join yarn, Work back and forth as for front until armhole measures 7½ (8, 8½, 9, 9½)", ending with a WS row. Place sts on holder. Leave yarn tail to BO shoulders as before; break yarn.

JOIN SHOULDERS

Turn piece inside out and arrange sts on two circ needles, one each for the front and back sts. Using the tail of

Berkshire Pullover in natural with Brioche Hat (page 62) in twilight green and old sage.

yarn, work three-needle bind-off as follows: Insert a dpn into the first st on each of the other two needles and knit them together as one st, *knit the next st on each needle together in the same way (2 sts on right-hand needle), pass the first st on right-hand needle over the second to BO; repeat from * until 12 (14, 16, 18, 20) sts have been bound off—1 st remains on right-hand needle. Fasten off last st on right-hand needle. Slide sts to other end of circ needles, and BO 12 (14, 16, 18, 20) sts from the opposite side for other shoulder—36 (36, 36, 36, 38) live sts remain for neck; 18 (18, 18, 18, 19) sts each on front and back needles. Carefully turn piece right side out. Transfer all neck sts to shorter circ needle and join yarn at one shoulder seam. BO all sts around neck opening as if to knit, picking up and binding off 1 extra st at each shoulder seam. Fasten off last st.

SLEEVES (make 2)

Using dpn and beginning at underarm, pick up and knit 38 (40, 43, 45, 48) sts around armhole opening (approximately 1 st for every 2 rows of knitting, 1 extra st at underarm, and 1 extra st at shoulder seam). Place marker to indicate beginning of rnd. Work even in St st for 8 rnds. Next rnd: K2tog, knit to last 2 sts, k2tog—2 sts decreased. Repeat the last 9 rnds 7 (7, 7, 7, 8) times—22 (24, 27, 29, 30) sts. Work even until sleeve measures 16½ (17, 18, 18½, 19)" from armhole, or desired length. BO all sts. Repeat for other sleeve

FINISHING

Block lightly, if desired.

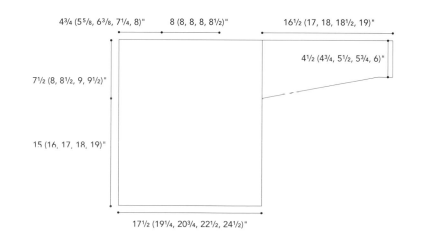

4¾ (5⅝, 6⅜, 7¼, 8)" 　 8 (8, 8, 8, 8½)" 　 16½ (17, 18, 18½, 19)"

4½ (4¾, 5½, 5¾, 6)"

7½ (8, 8½, 9, 9½)"

15 (16, 17, 18, 19)"

17½ (19¼, 20¾, 22½, 24½)"

The Berkshire Pullover in hemlock and oatmeal.

bergamo

cache-coeur

VÉRONIK AVERY

Cache-Coeur (rhymes with *wash-her*) literally translates from French as "hide the heart" and is used in the French dance world to describe the crossover tops ballerinas wear. Designer Véronik Avery, who is French-Canadian, borrowed the romantic term for this short vest that, she says, both hides and warms the heart. (In a 19th-century knitting book, I found a vest similar to this one identified as a hug-me-tight.) Bergamo is the name of the tubular wool ribbon with which the vest is made.

Finished Measurements
33¾ (36¾, 40¼, 42¼, 44¾, 48¼, 50¾)" chest. Vest shown measures 36¾".

Yarn
Muench Bergamo (100% wool ribbon; 66 yards / 50 grams): 7 (7, 8, 9, 9, 10, 11) balls. Shown in #3902 red.

Needles
One 24" or longer circ (circular) needle size US 10½ (6.5 mm).
Three 24" or longer circ needles size US 9 (5.5 mm) for edging.
Change needle size if necessary to obtain the correct gauge.

Notions
Stitch holders, yarn needle, 2 yards thin smooth scrap yarn for provisional cast-on (optional).

Gauge
16 sts and 24 rows = 4" (10 cm) in Stockinette stitch (St st).

Review notes on page 80 before beginning to knit.

BACK
Using larger needle and provisional cast-on (see Notes) or other temporary cast-on of your choice, CO 55 (59, 67, 71, 75, 83, 87) sts. Purl 1 row, knit 1 row, purl 1 row. Change to purl dot pattern (see Notes) and work even in pattern until piece measures 2¾ (2¾, 2½, 2½, 2¼, 2, 1½)", ending with a WS row. Increase Row: K2, M1 (see Notes), work in pattern as established to last 2 sts, M1, k2—2 sts increased. Work 7 rows even in pattern. Working increased sts into pattern, repeat the last 8 rows 2 (2, 0, 0, 0, 0, 0) more times—61 (65, 69, 73, 77, 85, 89) sts. Work an increase row, then work 5 rows even. Repeat the last 6 rows 2 (2, 5, 3, 4, 3, 1) time(s)—67 (71, 81, 81, 87, 93, 93) sts. Work an increase row, then work 3 rows even. Repeat the last 4 rows 0 (0, 0, 3, 2, 4, 8) time(s)—69 (73, 83, 89, 93, 103, 111) sts. Work even in pattern until piece measures 10½ (10¾, 10¾, 10¾, 10¾, 11¼)" from beginning, ending with a WS row. Shape shoulders: (RS) Work in pattern until 5 (5, 3, 2, 1, 2, 3) sts remain at end of row, turn. Next row: Yo (see Notes), purl until 5 (5, 3, 2, 1, 2, 3) sts remain at end of row, turn. Work 6 (10, 12, 14, 16, 18, 18)

The twisted-cord tie is optional on this romantic vest.

notes

- **M1 (make 1):** Insert tip of left-hand needle under the strand between the two needles, from back to front, and lift this strand onto the left-hand needle. Knit the lifted strand through the front of loop to increase 1 st.

- **Yo (yarnover):** Bring yarn to the front and over the right needle. Work the newly-created loop as a st on the next row.

- **Ssk (slip, slip, knit):** Slip the next 2 sts to right needle one at a time as if to knit, pass them back to left-hand needle one at a time in their new orientation and knit them together through the back of their loops.

- The short-row shaping for this project creates gaps in the work where it is turned. To close a gap when a yo precedes it, work to the yo, then k2tog (the yo and the next st after it). To close a gap when a yo follows it, work to 1 st before the gap, then ssk (the stitch before the gap and the yo after it).

- **Backward Loop Cast-On:** Make a loop in the working yarn and place on the right-hand needle, oriented so that it doesn't unwind, to increase 1 st.

- **Purl Dot Pattern (multiple of 4 stitches, plus 3)**
  ROW 1: (RS) K3, *p1, k3; repeat from * to end.
  ROWS 2, 4, AND 6: Purl all sts.
  ROWS 3 AND 7: Knit all sts.
  ROW 5: K1, *p1, k3; repeat from * to last 2 sts, end p1, k1.
  ROW 8: Purl all sts.
  Repeat Rows 1–8 for pattern.

- **Provisional Cast-On:** Using a thin, smooth scrap yarn, CO the required number of sts and work in Stockinette st (St st) for 3–4 rows. Change to main yarn and continue as directed.

- **Kitchener Stitch:** On a yarn needle, thread a length of yarn approximately 4 times the length of the section to be joined. Hold needles with sts to be grafted with purl sides of work together. Working from right to left, *insert yarn needle in first stitch on front needle as if to knit, pull yarn through, remove st from needle. Insert yarn needle into next st on front needle as if to purl, pull yarn through, leave st on needle. Insert yarn needle into first st on back needle as if to purl, pull yarn through, remove st from needle. Insert yarn needle into next st on back needle as if to knit, pull yarn through, leave st on needle. Repeat from * until 1 st remains on each needle. Cut yarn and pass through last 2 sts to fasten off.

rows as follows: Yo, work in pattern until 4 sts remain before previous gap (not counting yo's), turn. For all sizes *except* 36¾", work two more rows as follows: Yo, work until 6 (0, 2, 2, 1, 1, 2) sts remain before gap, turn, yo, purl until 6 (0, 2, 2, 1, 1, 2) sts remain before gap, turn. For all sizes, next row: Yo, work to end of row, closing all gaps as given in Notes. Purl 1 row across all sts, closing any remaining gaps as before—69 (73, 83, 89, 93, 103, 111) sts. Place sts on a holder.

RIGHT FRONT

Using larger needles and provisional cast-on or other temporary cast-on of your choice, CO 19 (23, 26, 28, 31, 34, 37) sts.
ROW 1: (WS) P15 (19, 22, 24, 27, 30, 33) sts, turn (4 sts left unworked at end of needle).
ROW 2: Yo, knit to end.
ROW 3: P15 (19, 22, 24, 27, 30, 33) sts, close gap as given in Notes, p1, turn (2 sts left unworked at end of needle).
ROW 4: Yo, k1 (1, 0, 1, 1, 0, 0), *p1, k3; repeat from * 4 (5, 6, 6, 7, 8, 8) times, end p0 (0, 0, 1, 0, 0, 1), k0 (0, 0, 0, 0, 0, 2). This establishes Row 1 of purl dot pattern.
ROW 5: P17 (21, 24, 26, 29, 32, 35), close gap, purl to end. This counts as Row 2 of purl dot pattern.

Continue in purl dot pattern as established until piece measures 2¾ (2¾, 2½, 2½, 2¼, 2, 1½)", ending with a WS row. (Note: The later steps of the side shaping and the front neck shaping happen at the same time. Please read through the instructions carefully up to the shoulder shaping before proceeding.) Increase Row: (RS) Work in pattern to last 2 sts, M1, k2—1 st increased at side edge. Work

7 rows even in pattern. Working increased sts into pattern, repeat the last 8 rows 2 (2, 0, 0, 0, 0, 0) times. Work an increase row, then work 5 rows even. Repeat the last 6 rows 2 (2, 5, 3, 4, 3, 1) time(s). Work an increase row, then work 3 rows even. Repeat the last 4 rows 0 (0, 0, 3, 2, 4, 8) time(s). *And at the same time*, when piece measures 7½ (7¾, 8, 8¼, 8½, 8½, 8¾)" from beginning, shape neck by decreasing at beginning of RS rows as follows: K1, ssk at neck edge, work in pattern to end, making any necessary increases at side edge. Decrease at neck edge in this manner every 6 (4, 2, 2, 2, 2, 2) rows 0 (4, 1, 2, 4, 3, 7) times, then every 8 (6, 4, 4, 4, 4, 4) rows 2 (0, 3, 2, 1, 1, 0) times—23 (25, 29, 32, 34, 39, 41) sts remain after all side shaping and neck decreases have been completed. Work even until piece measures 10½ (10¾, 10¾, 10¾, 10¾, 10¾, 11¼)", ending with a WS row.

Shape shoulders: (RS) Work in pattern until 5 (5, 3, 2, 1, 2, 3) sts remain at end of row, turn, yo, purl to end, turn. Next row: *Work in pattern until 4 sts remain before previous gap (not counting yo's), turn; yo, purl to end; repeat from * 3 (5, 6, 7, 8, 9, 9) times total. For all sizes *except 36¾"*, work two more rows as follows: Work until 6 (0, 2, 2, 1, 1, 2) sts remain before gap, turn, yo, purl to end, turn. For all sizes, next row: Work to end of row, closing all gaps as given in Notes.

Purl 1 row across all sts, closing any remaining gaps as before—23 (25, 29, 32, 34, 39, 41) sts. Place sts on a holder.

LEFT FRONT

Using larger needles and provisional cast-on or other temporary cast-on of your choice, CO 19 (23, 26, 28, 31, 34, 37) sts.

ROW 1: (WS) Purl all sts.
ROW 2: K15 (19, 22, 24, 27, 30, 33) sts, turn (4 sts left unworked at end of needle).
ROW 3: Yo, purl to end.
ROW 4: K15 (19, 22, 24, 27, 30, 33) sts, close gap as given in Notes, k1, turn (2 sts left unworked at end of needle).
ROW 5: Yo, purl to end.
ROW 6: P0 (0, 0, 1, 0, 0, 0), k3 (3, 3, 3, 3, 3, 2), p1, *k3, p1; repeat from * 3 (4, 5, 5, 6, 7, 8) times, k1 (1, 0, 1, 1, 0, 0), close gap, knit to end. This establishes Row 1 of purl dot pattern.

Continue in purl dot pattern as established until piece measures 2¾ (2¾, 2½, 2½, 2¼, 2, 1½)", ending with a WS row. Complete as for right front, reversing shaping. To shape sides, work increases at beginning of RS rows as follows: K2, M1, work in pattern to end of row. To shape front neck, work decreases at the end of RS rows as follows: Work in pattern to last 3 sts, k2tog, k1. When piece measures 10½ (10¾, 10¾, 10¾, 10¾, 10¾, 11¼)", ending with a RS row, shape shoulders: (WS) Purl until

5 (5, 3, 2, 1, 2, 3) sts remain at end of row, turn, yo, work in pattern to end, turn. Next row: *Purl until 4 sts remain before previous gap (not counting yo's), turn; yo, work in pattern to end; repeat from * 3 (5, 6, 7, 8, 9, 9) times total. For all sizes *except 36¾"*, work two more rows as follows: Purl until 6 (0, 2, 2, 1, 1, 2) sts remain before gap, turn, yo, work in pattern to end, turn. For all sizes, next row: Purl to end of row, closing all gaps as given in Notes. Work 1 row across all sts, closing any remaining gaps as before—23 (25, 29, 32, 34, 39, 41) sts. Place sts on a holder.

SIDE BANDS

Using yarn needle, graft live sts together at shoulders using Kitchener stitch (see Notes). With smaller needle and RS facing, beginning at bottom of left front, pick up and knit 46 sts along side edge of left front to shoulder seam as follows: Pick up 40 sts at a rate of approximately 2 sts for every 3 rows (pick up in two consecutive rows, then skip a row), then pick up 6 sts at a rate of 1 st for every 2 rows (pick up in 1 row, skip the next row). With the same needle, pick up and knit 46 sts from shoulder seam along side edge of left back as follows: Pick up 6 sts at a rate of 1 st for every 2 rows, then pick up 40 sts at a rate of approximately 2 sts for every 3 rows—92 sts on needle. Knit 3 rows.

ROW 1: (RS) *Insert right-hand needle tip into st, wrap yarn four times around needle, and pull through, keeping all wraps on needle; repeat from * to end.
ROW 2: Slip 4 sts (16 wraps) as if to purl with yarn in back, dropping the 3 extra wraps of each st to convert it

I mean that my heart unto yours is knit, so that but one heart we can make of it.

From *A Midsummer Night's Dream*, WILLIAM SHAKESPEARE

into a single, elongated st. Return the 4 elongated sts to left-hand needle and insert tip of right-hand needle into the front of the third and fourth sts from right to left, then pass them over first 2 sts without removing any sts from left-hand needle (the third and fourth sts will now be the first sts on the left-hand needle). Knit the 4 sts in their new order. *Slip 8 sts (32 wraps), dropping extra wraps as before. Return the 8 elongated sts to left-hand needle and pass last 4 sts over first 4, without removing them from the needle as before. Knit these 8 sts in their new order. Repeat from * to end of row.

Knit 3 rows. BO and join side seams as follows: Transfer half the sts to another smaller circular needle. Fold work in half with right sides together. Beginning at lower edge, BO the first 12 (12, 11, 11, 10, 8, 7) sts of front and back together as follows: Using a third smaller circ needle, insert tip of needle into first st on both front and back needles and k2tog (1 st from each needle), *k2tog

the next st from each needle—2 sts on right-hand needle. BO 1 st. Repeat from * until 12 (12, 11, 11, 10, 8, 7) sts each from front and back have been bound off together. BO remaining sts in the usual manner around armhole opening.

Repeat edging for right side, beginning the pickup at lower right back, and placing the 4-st cross on the back by working it at the end of Row 2, instead of at the beginning. BO side seams and armhole as for left side.

FRONT OPENING
Use as many smaller circ needles as necessary to comfortably hold all the sts. With RS facing, beginning at lower right side seam, pick up and knit 2 sts from side band, CO 2 sts directly above the cross st using backward loop cast-on, pick up and knit 2 sts from side band, carefully remove the provisional cast-on, pick up and knit 20 (23, 25, 29, 31, 34, 37) along bottom edge of right front, pick up and knit 48 (52, 53, 54, 55, 57, 57) along right front opening, pick

up and knit 23 (23, 25, 25, 25, 25, 29) sts across back neck, pick up and knit 48 (52, 53, 54, 55, 57, 57) along left front opening, carefully remove provisional cast-on, pick up and knit 20 (23, 25, 29, 31, 34, 37) along bottom edge of left front, pick up and knit 2 sts from side band, CO 2 sts above cross st as before, pick up and knit 4 sts from bands at left side seam (2 from each band), CO 2 sts above cross st, carefully remove provisional cast-on, pick up and knit 2 sts from back band, pick up and knit 57 (59, 67, 73, 75, 81, 87) across lower back, pick up and knit 2 sts from band, CO 2 st above cross, pick up and knit 2 sts from band—240 (256, 272, 288, 296, 312, 328) sts on needles. Knit 3 rows.
ROW 1: (RS) *Insert right-hand needle tip into st, wrap yarn four times around needle, and pull through, keeping all wraps on needle; repeat from * to end.
ROW 2: *Slip 8 sts as if to purl with yarn in back, dropping extra wraps. Return the 8 elongated sts to left-hand needle and pass last 4 sts over first 4, without removing them from the needle. Knit these 8 sts in their new order. Repeat from * to end of row. Knit 3 rows. BO all sts.

BLOCKING AND FINISHING
Hand wash garment in lukewarm water and pin to finished measurements. Air-dry. Optional ties: If desired, make two 9" lengths of twisted cord (as for Checkers Tote drawstring, see page 54), and attach one to the edging pickup row inside each front, at the beginning of neck shaping.

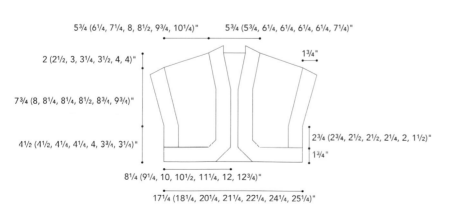

5³/₄ (6¹/₄, 7¹/₄, 8, 8¹/₂, 9³/₄, 10¹/₄)"   5³/₄ (5³/₄, 6¹/₄, 6¹/₄, 6¹/₄, 6¹/₄, 7¹/₄)"

2 (2¹/₂, 3, 3¹/₄, 3¹/₂, 4, 4)"   1³/₄"

7³/₄ (8, 8¹/₄, 8¹/₄, 8¹/₂, 8³/₄, 9³/₄)"

4¹/₂ (4¹/₂, 4¹/₄, 4¹/₄, 4, 3³/₄, 3¹/₄)"   2³/₄ (2³/₄, 2¹/₂, 2¹/₂, 2¹/₄, 2, 1¹/₂)"   1³/₄"

8¹/₄ (9¹/₄, 10, 10¹/₂, 11¹/₄, 12, 12³/₄)"

17¹/₄ (18¹/₄, 20¹/₄, 21¹/₄, 22¹/₄, 24¹/₄, 25¹/₄)"

perfect pie shawl

shawl

VÉRONIK AVERY

Wear this fluffy mohair shawl—which is a half-pie shape when opened up wide—tied in front, tied in back, or wrapped around itself (as shown here). It's knitted in a basic corded rib stitch with short rows for shaping. The body of the shawl is knitted on big needles in mohair and is contrasted beautifully with the dainty edging worked on smaller needles in a fine, shiny Merino wool. Inspiration for the edging, which is optional, came from a photograph of a chic-looking woman wearing a lacy shawl in *Marie Claire Idées*, a beautiful French craft magazine worth looking at even if you can't read French.

Review notes on page 86 before beginning to knit.

SHAWL

Using circ needle, CO 76 sts loosely.
ROW 1: Ssk, M1 (see Notes), p2, turn.
ROW 2 (and all even numbered rows): Yo (see Notes), *ssk, M1, p2; repeat from * to end.
ROW 3: Ssk, M1, p2, sssk (the yo of the previous row and next 2 sts; see Notes), M1, p2, turn.
ROW 5: [Ssk, M1, p2] 2 times, sssk, M1, p2, turn.
ROW 7: [Ssk, M1, p2] 3 times, sssk, M1, p2, turn.
Continue in pattern as established, working the 4-st repeat one more time every odd-numbered row, until all sts have been worked, ending with an odd-numbered row—76 sts, 37 rows completed.

Finished Measurements
Approximately 48" wide by 24" high at deepest point, after blocking.

Yarn
Shawl body: Berroco Mohair Classic / Berroco Mohair Classic Heather (78% mohair, 13% wool, 9% nylon; 93 yards / 42 grams): 5 balls. Shown in #1138 blue and #A9541 green heather.

Shawl edging: Koigu Premium Merino (100% wool; 175 yards / 50 grams): picot edging, 1 ball, shown in #2171 blue; rickrack lace, 2 balls, shown in #2340 green.

Needles
One 32" circular (circ) needle size US 10 (6.5 mm) for shawl body. One set straight needles size US 3 (3.25 mm) for edging. Change needle size if necessary to obtain correct gauge.

Notions
Stitch holders, stitch markers, yarn needle, crochet hook size H/5 (5 mm) for picot edging (optional), 1–2 yards of smooth, thin scrap yarn for rickrack lace cast-on (optional).

Gauge
Using larger needle, 14 sts and 19 rows = 4" in lace pattern, after blocking.

Perfect Pie Shawl with picot edging over Cashmere Pullover (page 68) and Look-Back Leggings worn as arm warmers (page 124).

notes

- The wedge-shaped lace sections of the shawl are worked using short rows. All the stitches for each section of the pie are cast on first. Then the stitches are worked back and forth in short rows, working increasingly more stitches according to the pattern instructions, until all stitches in the section have been worked. Then the process is reversed, working increasingly fewer stitches according to the pattern.

- **Ssk (slip, slip, knit):** Slip the next 2 sts to right-hand needle one at a time as if to knit, pass them back to left-hand needle one at a time in their new orientation and knit them together through the back of their loops.

- **Sssk (slip, slip, slip, knit):** Slip the next 3 sts to right-hand needle one at a time as if to knit, pass them back to left-hand needle one at a time in their new orientation and knit them together through the back of their loops.

- **M1 (make 1):** With the tip of the left-hand needle inserted from front to back, lift the strand between the two needles onto the left-hand needle and knit it. Do not twist the M1 loop as you work it; for this pattern it is deliberately supposed to make a decorative hole.

- **Yo (at beginning of a row):** Bring yarn to the front of needle with no stitches, insert needle into first st to be worked. If the first stitch to be worked is a knit stitch, bring yarn around to back and k1; if the first stitch to be worked is a purl stitch, bring yarn around to back, then between the needles to the front, and p1.

- **Crochet slipstitch (sl st):** Insert hook into stitch, yarn over hook and draw through stitch and loop on hook.

- **Chain stitch (ch):** *Yarn over hook, draw through loop on hook; rep from * for number of times instructed.

- **Provisional Cast-On:** Using a thin, smooth scrap yarn, CO the required number of sts and work in Stockinette st (St st) for 3 – 4 rows. Change to main yarn and continue as directed.

ROW 38: [Ssk, M1, p2] 19 times (Note: there is no yo at the beginning of this even-numbered row).

ROW 39: [Ssk, M1, p2] 18 times, turn.

ROW 40 AND ALL EVEN-NUMBERED ROWS: Yo, *(ssk, M1, p2); repeat from * to end.

ROW 41: [Ssk, M1, p2] 17 times.

Continue in pattern as established, working the 4-st repeat one less time every odd-numbered row, until you have completed a row in which only 4 sts have been worked. Work 1 even-numbered row as established—74 rows and one wedge section have been completed.

TRANSITION ROWS
(worked between wedge sections)

ROW 1: Ssk, M1, p2, *sssk (yo of previous row and next 2 sts), M1, p2; repeat from * to end—76 sts.

ROW 2: *Ssk, M1, p2; repeat from * to end.

Continue as for the first wedge section, beginning with Row 1, working 1 additional 4-st repeat on every odd-numbered row through Row 37, then working 1 less 4-st repeat through Row 74, and ending with another pair of transition rows. Continue in this manner until a total of 5 wedge sections have been completed,

ending with Row 74 of the 5th wedge. Work transition Row 1 once more—76 sts. BO all sts loosely.

FINISHING

With yarn threaded on a yarn needle, weave in ends. Work picot or rickrack lace edging as desired. The shawl also works equally well without an edging.

PICOT EDGING

Join edging yarn to one corner of shawl, and using crochet hook, *work 1 crochet sl st (see Notes) in next edge st of shawl, ch 3 (see Notes), work 1 sl st into st at base of 3-st ch; repeat from * around. Join last st to beginning with a sl st. Cut yarn and draw through last loop to secure.

RICKRACK LACE

Using the provisional cast-on (see Notes), or other temporary cast-on of your choice, and smaller needles, CO 7 sts. Next row: K2, p5. Beginning at one corner of the long top edge, continue rickrack lace, attaching to the long top edge of shawl approximately every 1½" as follows:

ROW 1 (RS): Using tip of right-hand needle or crochet hook, pull the first st of lace row through next edge st of shawl and replace it on the left-hand needle; k1, [ssk, yo] twice, k2.

ROW 2 AND ALL EVEN-NUMBERED ROWS: K2, p5.

ROWS 3, 5 AND 7: K1, [ssk, yo] twice, k2.

ROWS 9, 11, AND 13: K2, [yo, k2tog] twice, k1.

ROW 15: Join first st to shawl as in Row 1, approximately 1½" away from previous join, k1, (yo, k2tog) twice, k1.

ROW 16: K2, p5.

Repeat these 16 rows for pattern. In other words, after joining the edging to the shawl in Row 15, work Row 16, then work Row 1 of the next repeat, joining the edging to the very next shawl st after the one joined in Row 15. Work edging Rows 2–14 as given above, without joining, then join edging to shawl in Row 15, approximately 1½" away from the st joined in Row 1. Work edging in this manner around the entire edge of the shawl, ending with Row 16. As you approach the corner, adjust the placement of the joins on the shawl edge, if necessary, so that the join in Row 15 of the last repeat ends

in the corner st of shawl. Turn the corner as follows:

ROW 1: K2, p4, turn.

ROW 2 AND ALL EVEN-NUMBERED ROWS: Knit.

ROW 3: K2, p3, turn.

ROW 5: K2, p2, turn.

ROW 7: K2, p1, turn.

ROW 9: K2, turn.

ROW 11: K1, p1, turn

Continue in this manner, working 1 more purl st in each odd-numbered row, until all sts have been worked, ending with a WS row—7 sts.

Beginning with Row 1, continue rickrack edging around the rest of the

shawl, joining as before, until you reach the provisional cast-on edge. As you approach the corner where you began, adjust the placement of the joins on the shawl edge, if necessary, so that the join in Row 15 of the last repeat ends in the corner st of shawl. Turn the second corner same as the first. Carefully remove the provisional cast-on yarn from beginning of rickrack edging by cutting it in 3–4 places (being careful not to cut lace yarn), and gently pulling the cut pieces free. Place live loops on needle. Graft or sew live sts at ends of edging together. Block to finished measurements.

The rickrack lace edging on this shawl is more elaborate than the picot edging on the blue one on page 85.

union square shawl/poncho

I wore a shawl like this to New York City's annual Knit-Out, an autumn gathering of thousands of knitters in Union Square, and received so many compliments from people of every age group that I decided to include a new version of it here. The one I wore featured a basic 4-by-4 rib and came from *Rebecca*, the German pattern magazine. For this version, I added the baby cable in the knitted part of the rib and made the neck opening slightly smaller.

This is a great project to work on during a long car trip or while watching television or chatting with friends. First, it requires no shaping—you simply knit a long rectangle then sew it together strategically to create the poncholike shape. Second, the stitch pattern is easy to memorize within the first few rows since all the rows are basically the same except for every fourth row, in which the baby cable is formed by twisting two stitches around each other.

Wear this garment with the point in front and it looks like a poncho; wear it with the straight section in front and it looks more like a shawl; or wear it somewhere in between—whatever feels most comfortable.

Finished Measurements
19" wide by 54" long, before seaming, lightly blocked.

Yarn
GGH Via Mala (100% Merino wool; 73 yards / 50 grams): 12 balls. Shown in #16 gray.

Needles
One 29" or longer circ (circular) needle size US 9 (5.5 mm). Change needle size if necessary to obtain the correct gauge.

Notions
Yarn needle, T-pins for blocking, removable stitch marker or safety pin for marking sewing position.

Gauge
19 sts and 22 rows = 4" in baby cable rib pattern, lightly blocked.

Review notes on page 91 before beginning to knit.

SHAWL/PONCHO

CO 90 sts. Work in baby cable ribbing until piece measures 54" or desired length from beginning, and end having just completed Row 2. BO all sts. Block by pinning piece to measurements, spraying lightly with water, and leaving to dry.

FINISHING

Mark corners A, B, and C as shown on diagram, with corners A and B at the BO edge. Mark position D, 20" up from CO edge as shown. With RS facing, pin corner B to marked position D, then pin corner A to corner C, and stretching BO edge slightly to fit. With yarn threaded on a yarn needle, sew seam from A/C to B/D. Weave in ends.

Sewing Shawl/Poncho

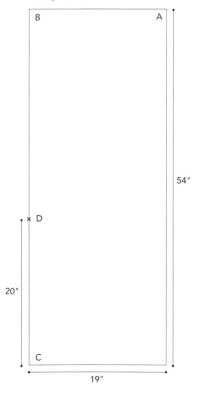

notes

- For neat edges, sl (slip) the first st of every row as if to purl with yarn in front, and knit the last st of every row.

- **Baby Cable Ribbing (multiple of 4 stitches, plus 2)**
  ROWS 1 AND 3: (WS) Sl 1 as if to purl with yarn in front, k1, *p2, k2; rep from * to end.
  ROW 2: (RS) Sl 1 as if to purl with yarn in front, p1, *k2, p2; rep from * to last 4 sts, end k2, p1, k1.
  ROW 4: Sl 1 as if to purl with yarn in front, p1; *k2tog but leave both sts on left-hand needle, insert right-hand needle between 2 sts just knitted together and knit the first stitch again, sl both sts from needle together; p2; rep from * to last 4 sts; k2tog but leave both sts on left needle, insert right-hand needle between 2 sts just knitted together and knit the first stitch again, sl both sts from needle together; p1, k1.
  Repeat Rows 1 – 4 for pattern.

and pull-off cowl

fluffy lace camisole

ALISSA BAPTISTA

This ultra-feminine lace camisole, knitted in a fluffy mohair-silk yarn, works as an undergarment or an outer garment. The cowl, an optional addition, can also be worn as a scarf with a coat. Alissa Baptista got the cowl idea from the Russian women she met while working in a yarn shop in New York City. They wore cowls under their coats on cold days.

Review notes on page 94 before beginning to knit.

Camisole

LOWER BODY
With longer circ needle, CO 145 (161, 177, 193) sts. Join for working in the rnd (round), being careful not to twist sts, and pm (place marker) for beginning of rnd. Work even in Lace Pattern in the Round (see Notes), beginning with Rnd 1, until piece measures 12½ (14, 15½, 16)" from beginning, ending with Rnd 2 or 4, and pm after st 73 (81, 89, 97) on the last rnd—145 (161, 177, 193) sts total, 73 (81, 89, 97) sts for back, 72 (80, 88, 96) sts for front.

DIVIDE FOR FRONT AND BACK
Change to Lace Pattern in Rows (work back and forth). Remove beginning m (marker) and BO 6 sts— 1 st on right-hand needle after completing BO's. Counting the st on the right-hand needle as the first k1 of the row, work Row 1 of pattern until 4 sts before next marker, k4. Place sts just worked on a holder for back, being careful to keep all yarnovers in their proper positions. Remove marker and BO the first 5 sts of front—1 st on right needle after completing BO's. Counting the first st

Finished Measurements
38 (42½, 46½, 50¾)" chest. Camisole shown measures 38".

Yarn
Camisole and cowl body: Rowan Kidsilk Haze (70% super kid mohair, 30% silk; 229 yards / 25 grams): 2 (3, 3, 4) balls. Shown in #591 pale blue.
Camisole and cowl edging: DMC Cotton Perle (100% cotton; 27.3 yards / 5 grams): 3 skeins. Shown in #800 light blue.

Needles
One 24" circular (circ) needle size US 10 (6 mm) for camisole.
One 16" circ needle size US 10 (6 mm) for cowl.
Change needle size if necessary to obtain the correct gauge

Notions
Stitch markers, stitch holder, crochet hook size C (2.75 mm), yarn needle.

Gauge
19 sts = 5", and 17 rows/rounds = 4" in lace pattern, after blocking.

notes

- **Yo (yarnover):** Bring yarn to the front and over the right-hand needle. Work the newly-created loop as a st on the next row.

- **Psso (pass slipped stitch over):** Pass slipped st on right-hand needle over the sts indicated in the instructions, as in binding off.

- All sl (slipped) stitches are slipped as if to purl with the yarn in back.

- **Lace Pattern in the Round (odd number of stitches)**
  RND 1: K1, * yo (see above), sl 1, k1, yo, psso (pass slipped st over the knit st and yo just worked; see above); rep from * to end.
  RND 2: K1, *drop yo from needle, k2; rep from * to end.
  RND 3: K2, *yo, sl 1, k1, yo, psso; rep from *, end k1.
  RND 4: K2, * drop yo from needle, k2; rep from * to last st, k1.
  Repeat Rounds 1 – 4 for pattern.

- **Lace Pattern in Rows (multiple of 2 sts + 1)**
  ROW 1: (RS) K1, *yo, sl 1, k1, yo, psso; rep from * end.
  ROW 2: *P2, drop yo from needle; rep from *, end p1.
  ROW 3: K2, *yo, sl 1, k1, yo, psso; rep from *, end k1.
  ROW 4: P1, *p2, drop yo from needle; rep from *, end p2.
  Repeat Rows 1 – 4 for pattern.

- **Single Crochet:** Insert hook into edge st of garment and draw up a loop, *insert hook into next st and draw up a loop, yarn over hook, and draw through both loops on hook; repeat from * to end.

on the right needle as the first k1 of Row 1, work Row 1 of pattern to last 4 sts, end k4. Turn.

FRONT

Working on front sts only, BO 4 sts at the beginning of the next row (WS), work Row 2 of pattern to end—63 (71, 79, 87) sts. Next row: BO 4 sts, work Row 3 of pattern to last 4 sts, end k4. Next row: BO 4 sts, work Row 4 of pattern to end—55 (63, 71, 79) sts.

SHAPE V-NECK

Mark the center st to indicate base of V-neck. Next row: BO 2 sts, work Row 1 of pattern to 2 sts before marked center st, k2, k center st, work in pattern to last 2 sts, end k2. Next row: BO 2 sts, work Row 2 of pattern to center st, join second ball of yarn, work center st together with next st as you work in pattern to end—25 (29, 33, 37) sts each side. Working each side separately, BO 2 sts at each armhole edge once more, and at the same time dec 1 st at each neck edge every row 8 (12, 16, 20) times, ending with Row 2 or Row 4 of pattern—15

O, snugged in the valley,

A homestead of hearts!

Love flies like a shuttle

And knits while it darts.

Herman Melville

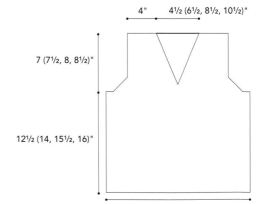

4"   4½ (6½, 8½, 10½)"

7 (7½, 8, 8½)"

12½ (14, 15½, 16)"

19 (21¼, 23¼, 25³⁄₈)"

sts remain for each shoulder. Note: If there are not enough sts to work a complete multiple of the pattern, work any sts outside the pattern in St st. Work even in pattern until armhole measures 7 (7½, 8, 8½)", ending with Row 2 or Row 4 of pattern. BO shoulder sts loosely.

BACK

Return back sts to needle, and join yarn ready to work a WS row. BO 4 sts at the beginning of the next row, work Row 2 of pattern to end—63 (71, 79, 87) sts. Next row: BO 4 sts, work Row 3 of pattern to last 4 sts, end k4. Next row: BO 4 sts, work Row 4 of pattern to end—55 (63, 71, 79) sts. Work even in pattern until armhole measures 7 (7½, 8, 8½)", ending with Row 2 or Row 4 of pattern. BO all sts loosely.

FINISHING

Sew shoulder seams. Weave in all ends. Block to finished measurements. Using crochet hook, work 2 rows of single crochet (see Notes) around neck edge, armholes, and lower edge of camisole.

Cowl

Using shorter circ needles, CO 133 sts. Join for working in the rnd, being careful not to twist sts, and pm for beginning of rnd. Work even in Lace Pattern in the Round, beginning with Rnd 1, until piece measures 12", ending with Rnd 2 or Rnd 4 of pattern. BO all sts loosely. Block and weave in all ends. Using crochet hook, work 2 rows of single crochet around CO and BO edges.

TAKING Tea

Drinking tea and knitting seem to go hand in hand, maybe because they're both about taking time out from the hubbub of everyday life and quieting down. Following are general guidelines for brewing a good pot.

- Fill the kettle with fresh, good-tasting cold water and set it on the stove to heat. If using tap water, let it run for a minute before filling the kettle.

- Heat the water to boiling if you are making black, dark oolong, or herbal tea; remove the kettle from the heat just before it boils if you are making green, light oolong, or white tea.

- While the water is heating, choose a favorite teacup or mug and set out any flavorings you want to use in the tea, such as milk, sugar, honey, lemon, or fruit jelly.

- Rinse the teapot with very hot water to warm it.

- Add the tea leaves to the pot in a tea ball or another type of infuser, or in bags. The amount of tea used depends on the amount of water, the kind of tea, and your individual taste. The general rule of thumb is one teaspoon for each serving of tea plus an extra teaspoon for the pot, or one teabag per serving. Experiment to figure out what works best for you.

- When ready, pour the water into the teapot and cover with the lid. Brew the tea for approximately 3 to 5 minutes. While the tea is brewing, warm your cup by rinsing it with very hot water.

- When the tea is ready, remove the leaves from the water. If you used teabags, squeeze all of the liquid out of them.

- Pour the tea through a strainer into your cup.

- Add flavorings, as desired.

- Sit back and savor.

fingerless mitts

ANN BUDD

I have been a fingerless glove and mitten devotee ever since I bought my first pair while traveling in the Shetland Islands. Sometimes I wear them on their own; sometimes I wear them on top of gloves. Either way, they allow the fingers lots of dexterity—and look really nice. I typed much of my first book, *Knitting in America*, wearing fingerless mitts. At the time, my husband was in graduate school, and he and I were living in a renovated barn we heated with wood. Because the barn was only minimally insulated, wearing the mitts was more necessity than fashion.

The mitts shown here (and on pages 99 and 100) are different from any others I've seen; because they are worked sideways, the garter ridges simulate ribs. Short rows are used to make the hand wider than the cuff. The thumb opening is worked like a large buttonhole—stitches are bound off on one row, then an equal number is cast on over the gap on the following row. Instead of a seam, the last row of knitting is worked together with stitches picked up from the cast-on row using a three-needle bind-off.

They make a perfect last-minute gift since they take only a few hours to complete. I made a pair for my husband one night and had them wrapped and ready to give to him in the morning. The instructions conveniently cover three gauges of yarn (4, 5, and 6 stitches to the inch) and three adult sizes.

Finished Sizes
About 6 (6½, 7)" hand circumference, measured around the base of the fingers. To fit woman's small/medium (woman's medium/large, man's small/medium) hand.

Yarn
4 stitches per inch: GGH Via Mala (100% Merino wool; 77 yards / 50 grams): 1 ball. Shown in #24 blue.
5 stitches per inch: Horstia Tweed (55% Merino wool, 27% acrylic, 18% viscose; 109 yards / 50 grams): 1 ball. Shown in #9 green.
6 stitches per inch: GGH Merino Soft (100% Merino wool; 186 yards / 50 grams): 1 (2, 2) balls (used double throughout). Shown in #70 rust.

Needles
One set straight needles in size necessary to obtain desired gauge. Change needle size if necessary to obtain the correct gauge.
Optional but helpful: A single needle several sizes smaller for picking up stitches along the cast-on edge.

Notions
Yarn needle.

Gauge
The following instructions are for gauges of 4, 5, and 6 stitches per inch in garter stitch.

notes

- **Long-tail Cast-On (also known as Continental Cast-On):** Leaving a tail with about 1" of yarn for each st to be cast-on, make a slipknot in the yarn and place it on the right-hand needle. Insert the thumb and forefinger of your left hand between the strands of yarn so the working end is around your forefinger, and the tail end is around your thumb "slingshot" fashion. Insert the tip of the right-hand needle into the loop on the thumb, hook the strand of yarn coming from the forefinger, and draw up a loop with the right-hand needle. Remove your thumb from the loop and pull on the working yarn to tighten the new stitch on the right-hand needle. Return your thumb and forefinger to their original positions, and repeat until you have cast on the number of stitches required.

- **Knitted Cast-On:** *Insert right-hand needle into last st on left-hand needle and draw up a loop. Place the loop on the left-hand needle. Repeat from * until you have cast on the number of stitches required.

To make mitts following this chart, choose your yarn, determine your gauge, and pick a size to match your hand size. The possible gauges (4, 5, or 6 stitches per inch) are listed vertically down the left side of the chart; the hand sizes are shown horizontally across the top.

FINISHED HAND CIRCUMFERENCE

6	6½	7"

Using the long-tail method (see Notes), CO

4 sts/in	24	26	28 sts.
5 sts/in	30	33	35
6 sts/in	36	39	42

Work garter st for

4 sts/in	5	3	5 rows.
5 sts/in	3	3	5
6 sts/in	3	3	3

Counting the ridge created on the WS by the CO, there will be the following number of garter ridges each on RS and WS:

4 sts/in	3	2	3
5 sts/in	2	2	3
6 sts/in	2	2	2

Work short row for hand as foll: Knit across

4 sts/in	11	12	13 sts,
5 sts/in	14	15	16
6 sts/in	16	18	20

Bring yarn to front, slip next st to right-hand needle, return yarn to back (to wrap st), return slipped st to left-hand needle, turn, work to end.

Note: Each short row will produce one more garter ridge on the hand edge (at the beginning of the needle on RS rows) than on the wrist edge (at the end of the needle on RS rows). On the following row, hide the wrap if desired by working the wrap together with the wrapped st.

Knit across all sts for

4 sts/in	8	10	10 rows.
5 sts/in	10	10	10
6 sts/in	10	10	10

There will be the following number of garter ridges at the wrist edge (end of RS rows):

4 sts/in	7	7	8
5 sts/in	7	7	8
6 sts/in	7	7	7

Work short row for hand as before. There will be 2 more garter ridges on the hand edge (beginning of RS rows) than at the wrist edge.

Knit all sts for

4 sts/in	0	0	0 rows.
5 sts/in	8	10	12
6 sts/in	8	10	12

There will be the following number of garter ridges at the wrist edge (end of RS rows):

4 sts/in	7	7	8
5 sts/in	11	12	14
6 sts/in	11	12	13

For gauges of 5 sts/in and 6 sts/in *only*, work short row for hand as before.

Knit across all sts for

4 sts/in	4	4	6 rows.
5 sts/in	2	2	2
6 sts/in	4	4	6

There will be the following number of garter ridges at the wrist edge (end of RS rows):

4 sts/in	9	9	11
5 sts/in	12	13	15
6 sts/in	13	14	16

THUMB

Knit across

4 sts/in	8	8	9 sts,
5 sts/in	11	11	11
6 sts/in	12	13	14

BO the following number of sts, then knit to end:

4 sts/in	3	4	4 sts
5 sts/in	3	4	5
6 sts/in	4	5	6

Knit 1 row, and at the same time, use the knitted method (see Notes) to CO the following number of sts over the gap formed in previous row:

4 sts/in	3	4	4 sts
5 sts/in	3	4	5
6 sts/in	4	5	6

Note: To make it easier to work the knitted CO, turn the work so the needle onto which you are working the CO sts is temporarily in your left hand. CO the required number of sts, then turn the work again to return the needle with the new sts to your right hand. As an option, you may also CO directly onto the right-hand needle without turning, using the backward loop method, but the CO edge of the thumb slit will not resemble the BO edge as closely as it will when using the knitted method.

Knit all sts for

4 sts/in	2	4	4 rows.
5 sts/in	4	6	8
6 sts/in	2	4	4

There will be the following number of garter ridges at the wrist edge (end of RS rows):

4 sts/in	11	12	14
5 sts/in	15	17	20
6 sts/in	15	17	19

For all gauges, work short row for hand as before.

Knit all sts for

4 sts/in	8	10	10 rows.
5 sts/in	10	10	10
6 sts/in	8	10	12

There will be the following number of garter ridges at the wrist edge:

4 sts/in	15	17	19
5 sts/in	20	22	25
6 sts/in	19	22	25

For all gauges, work short row for hand as before.

Knit all sts for

4 sts/in	0	0	0 rows.
5 sts/in	0	0	0
6 sts/in	10	10	10

He who works with his hands is a laborer.
He who works with his hands and his head is a craftsmen.
He who works with his hands, his head,
and his heart, is an artist.

St. Francis of Assisi

For gauge of 6 sts/in *only*, work short row for hand as before.

Knit all sts for

4 sts/in	5	5	5 rows,
5 sts/in	5	5	5
6 sts/in	5	5	5

ending at the wrist edge.

There will be the following number of garter ridges at the wrist edge:

4 sts/in	18	20	22 ridges.
5 sts/in	23	25	28
6 sts/in	27	30	33

There will be the following number of garter ridges at the hand edge:

4 sts/in	22	24	26 ridges.
5 sts/in	28	30	33
6 sts/in	33	36	39

FINISHING

With needle several sizes smaller (optional), pick up the following number of loops from CO edge:

4 sts/in	23	25	27 loops.
5 sts/in	29	32	34
6 sts/in	35	38	41

Hold the needle with the live sts so that the wrist edge is at the right-hand side of the needle; hold the needle with the picked-up sts parallel to and in front of the needle with the live sts. Use the three-needle method to bind off the sts together as follows: Slip the first live st from back needle onto an empty needle, *knit together one st from each of the two parallel needles, pass the first st over the second. Repeat from * until 1 st remains. Cut yarn and thread tail through remaining st. Make second mitt same as first. Weave in loose ends. Turn mitts right side out. Block lightly, if desired.

A GENTLE Hand Massage

I t's easy to get so motivated by progress on a knitting project—especially on a weekend when you have a large chunk of free time—that you don't want to stop even though your hands are feeling tired or sore, or your neck, shoulders, or another part of your body are tight. To soothe the hands and relax, take frequent breaks and give yourself a gentle hand massage. These reflexology techniques were shared with me by Karen Cornell-Froehner, a massage therapist in Dutchess County, New York.

- Remove all jewelry from hands or wrists before starting.

- To relax the neck and shoulders, shake the hands gently with hands in front of you, then above your head, then out to the side. Finish by hanging your hands down at your sides as you continue to shake them. Do this a few times.

- Cradle one hand inside the other. Using the thumb of the hand that is doing the cradling, begin to make small circular motions at the base of the thumb (the fat pad area) and into the web between the thumb and index finger. Work across the base of the finger pads, then toward the wrist down along the pinky-finger side of the hand. Repeat a few times on both hands.

- Repeat the hand-shaking sequence.

- Using your knuckles, massage the opposing hand up and down from the palm, into the wrist area, up to your elbow. You will begin to feel a tingling sensation run up your arms. Massage each hand and arm once. This relaxes the shoulder girdle, the rib cage area, lungs/chest, and heart.

- Cradle one hand in the other again. Using the thumb of the hand that is doing the cradling, massage just under the bottom knuckle joints on the palm side of the other hand (this is the diaphragm line), starting at the thumb and moving gently but firmly to the pinky. Repeat a few times, then change to the other hand.

- Rest one elbow on a desk or table. Intertwine your fingers into each other and begin to gently flex and extend the hand with the elbow on the surface. Repeat four times. Then, rotate the hand gently in a circular motion. Rotate to the right eight times, then repeat to the left. Repeat with the other elbow on the desk or table. This stretches the tendons of the arm.

- Repeat the hand-shaking sequence.

- Sweep the knuckles of your index and middle fingers down and up the palm of the other hand, working all the way to the edges of the hand, then up the arm. Repeat with the other hand.

- With a closed fist, using the heel of the hand, hit the base of the thumb several times. This will soften this thick tissue area. This aids in lower back issues.

- Finally, sweep your fingertips back and forth across the palms of your opposing hand (sweeping any tension away). Drop your hands to your sides and shake from side to side.

gloves and mittens

DEBORAH NEWTON

Use this versatile pattern to make gloves, fingerless gloves, or mittens. The garter-stitch cuff—worked in a solid color or in multiple colors—lends the otherwise classic design a new and interesting twist. The pattern also includes instructions for an optional loop at the edge of the cuff, a handy detail for folks who want to hang their gloves on a hook for safekeeping.

Review notes on page 105 before beginning to knit.

Gloves

CUFF
With color of your choice and larger dpn, CO 36 (40) sts. Divide evenly on 4 needles. Join, and pm (place marker) for beginning of rnd (round), taking care not to twist sts. *Knit 1 rnd, purl 1 rnd; repeat from * a total of 15 (18) times—15 (18) garter ridges.

LEFT GLOVE HAND
Next rnd: Knit around, increasing 3 sts evenly on each needle—48 (52) sts. Place a marker at the halfway point after 24 (26) sts. Work even in St st for 20 (22) rnds—glove measures approximately 2½ (2¾)" above the cuff.

LEFT GLOVE THUMB OPENING
Note: For the left glove the beginning of the rnd is at the pinky finger edge of the hand. Next rnd: K15 (16), k7

(8) thumb sts with an 8" piece of waste yarn, return last 7 (8) sts to left-hand needle, with main yarn k7(8) sts worked with waste yarn, k26 (28) to end. Thumb sts will be picked up from the waste yarn and worked later. Work

Finished Sizes
To fit woman's medium (man's medium). Finished hand circumference 8 (9)".

Yarn
Jaeger Matchmaker Merino DK (100% superwash wool; 131 yards / 50 grams). Solid gloves: 2 balls; fingerless gloves: 2 balls; mitten with multicolor cuffs: 2 balls main color (MC), 1 ball each of 2 contrasting colors (A and B). Shown in #866 blue, #868 purple rose, #877 gold.

Needles
One set of five double-pointed needles (dpn) size US 4 (3.5 mm).
Optional: Smaller set of dpn, size US 2 (2.5 mm) or US 3 (3.25), for tips of fingers and thumb.
Change needle size if necessary to obtain the correct gauge.

Notions
Stitch markers, stitch holders, yarn needle, small amount of waste yarn in contrasting color.

Gauge
Using larger dpn, 24 sts and 32 rounds = 4" in Stockinette stitch (St st) in the round.

Garter-Cuff Gloves with Lopi Lace Scarf (page 60).

notes

- **Ssk (slip, slip, knit):** Slip the next 2 sts to right-hand needle one at a time as if to knit, pass these 2 sts back to the left-hand needle one at a time in their new orientation, and knit them together through the back of their loops.

- **Backward Loop Cast-On:** Make a loop in the working yarn and place on the right-hand needle, oriented so that it doesn't unwind, to increase 1 st.

even in St st for 16 (18) rnds—glove measures approximately 2 (2¼)" above scrap yarn for thumb opening. Sl (slip) sts to 2 dpn, waste yarn, or holders, arranged 24 (26) sts for palm side of hand, and 24 (26) sts for back of hand.

THUMB

Sl a dpn into the 7 (8) sts below the thumb sts knitted with scrap yarn. Turn glove upside down to identify the loops at the top of the sts knitted with waste yarn and sl a dpn into the 6 (7) sts on the other side of thumb sts, plus 1 extra st at each end, for a total of 8 (9) sts on this dpn. Carefully remove the waste yarn—15 (17) sts total. Divide these sts over three dpn. Knit 1 rnd, *and at the same time*, pick up 1 st in each corner at base of thumb and knit this st through back of its loop to prevent forming a hole—17 (19) sts. Work even for 16 (18) rnds. Change to smaller dpn if desired, or work the thumb tip tightly as follows:

RND 1: K2tog around, end k1—9 (10) sts.

RND 2: Knit.

RND 3: K1 (0), k2tog around—5 sts. Cut yarn and draw through remaining sts to close thumb.

INDEX FINGER

Starting at the side of the hand above the thumb, place 6 (7) sts from palm and 6 (6) sts from back of hand on two larger dpns. Join yarn at palm side, and knit around, dividing sts over three dpn as you go, and using the backward loop method (see Notes), CO 3 (4) sts at end—15 (17) sts. Join for working in the rnd, and work even for 24 (27) rnds. Next rnd: K0 (1), k2tog around—12 (14) sts. Work 1 rnd even. Next rnd: K2tog around—6 (7) sts. Cut yarn and draw through remaining sts to close index finger.

PINKY FINGER

Starting at the opposite side of the hand, place 5 (5) sts from palm and 5 (6) sts from back on two larger dpns. Join yarn at back of hand side, and knit around, dividing sts over three dpn as you go, and, using the backward loop method, CO 2 (3) sts at end—12 (14) sts. Join for working in the rnd and work even for 16 (18) rnds. Next rnd: K2tog around—6 (7) sts. Work 1 rnd even. Next rnd: K0 (1), k2tog around—3 (4) sts. Cut yarn and draw through remaining sts to close pinky finger.

MIDDLE FINGER

Starting next to index finger, place 7 (7) sts from palm and 7 (7) sts from back on two larger dpns. Join yarn at palm side, k7, pick up 3 (4) sts at base of index finger, k7, then, using the backward loop method, CO 2 (3) sts, dividing sts over three dpn as you go— 19 (21) sts. Join for working in the rnd and knit 1 rnd, working k2tog at base of index finger on both palm and back of hand to close holes where fingers meet—17 (19) sts. Work even for 27 (30) rnds. Work tip as for thumb.

RING FINGER

Place remaining 6 (7) sts from palm and 6 (7) sts from back of hand on two larger dpn. Join yarn at palm side, k6 (7), pick up 4 (4) sts at base of middle finger, k6 (7), pick up 4 (4) sts at base of pinky finger, dividing sts over three dpn as you go—20 (22) sts. Join for working in the rnd and knit 1 rnd, working k2tog at base of pinky and middle fingers on both palm and back of hand to close holes where fingers meet—16 (18) sts. Work 2 rnds even, then dec 1 st on next rnd—15 (17) sts. Work even for 18 (21) rnds. Work tip as for index finger.

RIGHT GLOVE CUFF AND HAND

Work same as for left glove, placing thumb opening as follows: K24 (26) to halfway point of hand; k2, then k7 (8) with an 8" piece of waste yarn; knit to end. Complete hand and fingers as for left glove.

HANGING LOOP (optional)

With larger dpn, CO 20 sts. Knit 1 row. BO all sts on next row. Sew to lower edge at pinky side of hand as shown.

FINISHING

Weave in all ends firmly, closing any small holes, if necessary, at base of fingers and thumb.

Fingerless Gloves

Work same as for gloves, but when each finger and thumb measures approximately 1 (1¼)" to 1¼ (1½)", BO all sts. Work hanging loop, if desired, and finish as for gloves.

Mittens

To avoid seaming, the multicolored cuff may be worked in the rnd (round), as for gloves, but it requires carrying three yarns and twisting them on the WS of work at the beginning of each rnd. For an easier method, seamed cuff instructions are also provided.

CUFF IN THE ROUND

With larger dpn and A, CO 36 (40) sts. Divide evenly over 4 dpn. Join and pm (place marker) for beginning of rnd, taking care not to twist sts. *With A, knit 1 rnd, purl 1 rnd—1 garter ridge formed. Change to B and knit 1 rnd, purl 1 rnd. Change to MC and knit 1 rnd, purl 1 rnd. Repeat from * 4 (5) more times, ending with a MC rnd—15 (18) ridges.

SEAMED CUFF

This cuff is much quicker and easier. With A, CO 38 (42) sts. *With A, knit 2 rows—1 garter ridge formed. Change to B and knit 2 rows. Change to MC and knit 2 rows. Repeat from * 4 (5) times, decreasing 1 st at each end on last MC row—36 (40) sts; 15 (18) ridges. Arrange sts on four dpn, 9 (10) sts on each. Seam cuff, using 1 st at each side

as a seam st. From this point on, the mitten is worked in the rnd.

MITTEN LEFT HAND

Next rnd: With MC, knit around, increasing 3 sts evenly on each needle—48 (52) sts. Place a marker at the halfway point after 24 (26) sts. Work even in St st for 20 (22) rnds—mitten measures approximately 2½ (2¾)" above the cuff.

LEFT THUMB OPENING

Insert waste yarn for thumb as for left glove. Work even in St st for 34 (38) rnds or 2 (2¼)" less than desired length—mitten measures approximately 4¼ (4¾)" above waste yarn for thumb opening, or your chosen length.

MITTEN TIP

Decrease rnd: On first needle, k1, ssk (see Notes), knit to end; on second needle, knit to last 3 sts, k2tog, k1; on third needle, k1, ssk, knit to end; on fourth needle, knit to last 3 sts, k2tog, k1—4 sts decreased. Work 1 rnd even. Repeat the last 2 rnds until 20 sts remain, then work decrease rnd every rnd (omit the plain rnd), until 8 sts remain. Cut yarn and draw through remaining sts to close tip.

THUMB

Complete as for glove.

MITTEN RIGHT HAND

Work same as for left mitten, placing thumb opening as given in right glove instructions.

FINISHING

Weave in all ends firmly, closing any small holes, if necessary, at base of thumb.

As I was about leaving the forecastle,

I happened to look at my hands, and seeing them

stained all over of a deep yellow,

for that morning the mate had set me to tarring

some strips of canvas for the rigging,

I thought it would never do to present myself

before a gentleman that way;

so for want of kids, I slipped on

a pair of woolen mittens, which my mother

had knit for me to carry to sea . . . .

From *Redburn,*
HERMAN MELVILLE, 1847

super mittens

MARGRIT LOHRER

Knitted in a loosely twisted, bulky merino yarn, these mittens are super-soft, warm, and comfortable. They are knitted completely in Stockinette stitch with a long cuff section that keeps them in place without the usual ribbing. The optional crocheted chain that links the two mittens to each other (see photo on page 111) is a classic feature on children's mittens, but is a surprise—I think a delightful and practical one—as shown here in an adult size.

CUFF

CO 22 (26, 28, 30) sts. Join for working in the rnd (round), being careful not to twist sts, and pm (place marker) to indicate beginning of rnd. Work in St st for 14 (16, 18, 21) rnds, piece measures approximately 2½ (3, 3½, 4)" from beginning.

THUMB GUSSET

On the next rnd, begin shaping thumb gusset as follows: K1, pm, M1 (see page 34), k1, M1, pm, knit to end of rnd—2 sts increased; 3 sts between markers for thumb. Work 2 rnds even. Increase rnd: K1, sl m (slip marker), M1, knit to next marker, M1, slip marker, knit to end of rnd—2 sts increased. Work 2 rnds even. Repeat the last 3 rnds 1 (2, 3, 4) times—28 (34, 38, 42) sts; 7 (9, 11, 13) sts between markers

for thumb. Next rnd: K1, remove first marker, place next 7 (9, 11, 13) sts on holder for thumb, remove second marker, CO 1 st, knit to end—22 (26, 28, 30) sts.

Finished Size
To fit child's M/L (woman's S/M, woman's L/man's S, man's M/L). Finished hand circumference 6¼ (7½, 8, 8½)".

Yarn
Morehouse Merino Bulky (100% Merino wool; 102 yards / 4 oz). 1 skein. Shown in orange in size woman's S/M and in purple in size woman's L/man's S.

Needles
One set of five double-pointed needles (dpn) size US 10½ (6.5 mm). One set of five smaller dpn, size US 9 (5.5 mm) or US 10 (6 mm), for tip of both thumb and hand (optional).

Notions
Stitch markers, stitch holder, yarn needle, crochet hook size K (6.5 mm).

Gauge
Using larger dpn, 14 sts and 21 rounds = 4" in Stockinette stitch (St st) in the round. Change needle size if necessary to obtain the correct gauge.

But there is a more basic reason why people should knit. It has to do with respect for the gifts we have been given. These days our fingers are primarily trained to push buttons. When you see the speed and mastery with which they address computer keyboards, you know that fingers have enormous talents that are not being tapped. To leave your fingers untrained for anything beyond pushing. and perhaps twisting. is like leaving a voice without singing. It is a shame and a loss. Certainly knitting is not the only thing that fingers can do. but it is a good thing: simple yet capable of endless complexity.

From *Knitting for Anarchists*, ANNA ZILBOORG, 2002

HAND

Work 13 (14, 17, 19) rnds even, piece measures approximately 6¾ (8, 9½, 11)" from beginning. On the next rnd, begin shaping tip of mitten as follows (changing to smaller needles, if desired): *K2 tog; repeat from * to end—11 (13, 14, 15) sts. Work 1 rnd even. Next rnd: K1 (1, 0, 1), *k2tog; repeat from * to end—6 (7, 7, 8) sts. Break yarn, leaving an 8" tail. Draw through all sts and pull tight to close top of mitten.

THUMB

Arrange 7 (9, 11, 13) thumb sts on 2 needles, and join yarn with RS facing to beginning of first needle. With a third needle, pick up and knit 2 (2, 3, 3) sts at the base of the st CO over the thumb gap—9 (11, 14, 16) sts. Join for working in the rnd and pm to indicate beginning of rnd. Work even for 8 (9, 10, 12) rnds. Next rnd (changing to smaller needles, if desired): K1 (1, 0, 0), *k2tog; repeat from * to end—5 (6, 7, 8) sts. Break yarn, leaving an 8" tail. Draw through all sts and pull tight to close top of thumb. Make second mitten same as first.

FINISHING

Weave in all ends. Block lightly, or wash carefully on gentle cycle to slightly full (but not felt) the surface of the mittens. With crochet hook, make a crochet chain (see page 34) approximately 65" long. Attach to edge of mittens as shown.

notes

Central to the appeal
of knitting is that it wakes
like a meditation.
Everything becomes quiet,
still, and peaceful,
and all the turmoil of life
seems to succumb
to the silent rhythm of the
needles and the orderly
progression of the stitches.

From *The Principles of Knitting,*
June Hemmons Hiatt, 1988

SHAPE TOE

Beginning with the next color called for in the 2-rnd stripe sequence, stop working 2-rnd stripes, and instead work 1-rnd stripes in the following order: dark plum, magenta, grape. Decrease Rnd: On first needle, ssk (see Notes), work to end; on second needle, knit to last 2 sts, k2tog; on third needle ssk, work to end; on fourth needle, work to last 2 sts, k2tog—32 (36, 40) sts. Work 1 rnd even. Repeat the last 2 rnds 3 (4, 5) more times—20 sts. Knit 1 rnd. Slip sts from second needle onto first needle, and slip sts from fourth needle onto third needle—10 sts each on 2 needles. With the next color in the 1-rnd stripe order, use Kitchener stitch (see Notes) to graft remaining sts together.

HEEL

Carefully remove waste yarn and place sts from top and bottom of heel opening on 2 needles—36 (40, 44) sts. Using the color that doesn't match the stripes on either side of the heel opening, join yarn to one corner and work across all sts, picking up 1 extra st in each corner to close gaps—38 (42, 46) sts. Rearrange sts on four needles as follows: 9 (10, 11) sts on first and third needles, and 10 (11, 12) sts on second and fourth needles. Working 1-rnd stripes and decreases every other rnd as for toe, work until 4 (5, 6) decrease rnds have been completed—22 sts. Slip sts from second needle onto first needle, and slip sts from fourth needle onto third needle—11 sts each on 2 needles. With the next color in the 1-rnd stripe order, use Kitchener stitch to graft remaining sts together. Weave in ends. Make second sock same as first.

Solid Jazz Socks

CUFF

Using smaller needles CO 36 (40, 44) sts and divide evenly over four needles. Join for working in the rnd (round), being careful not to twist, and pm (place marker) for beginning of rnd. Next rnd: *K2, p2; repeat from * to end. Work 5 more rnds in k2, p2 rib as established. Change to larger needles and work in St st until piece measures 5½ (6, 6½)" from beginning, or desired length to anklebone. On the next rnd, work heel sts in waste yarn as follows: With contrasting waste yarn, knit 18 (20, 22) sts, drop the waste yarn, slide sts to beginning of needle where you started, and knit these sts again with main yarn, knit to end. Work even until piece measures 6½ (6¾, 7)" from waste yarn for heel, or 3 (3½, 4)" less than desired length (the toe and heel will each add 1½, 1¾, 2)" to the finished sock length).

SHAPE TOE

Decrease Rnd: On first needle, ssk (see Notes), work to end; on second needle, knit to last 2 sts, k2tog; on third needle ssk, work to end; on fourth needle, work to last 2 sts, k2tog–32 (36, 40) sts. Work 1 rnd even. Repeat the last 2 rnds 3 (4, 5) more times–20 sts. Knit 1 rnd. Slip sts from second needle onto first needle, and slip sts from fourth needle onto third needle–10 sts each on 2 needles. Use Kitchener stitch (see Notes) to graft remaining sts together.

HEEL

Carefully remove waste yarn and place sts from top and bottom of heel opening on 2 needles–36 (40, 44) sts. Join yarn to one corner and work across all sts, picking up 1 extra st in each corner to close gaps–38 (42, 46) sts. Rearrange sts on four needles as follows: 9 (10, 11) sts on first and third needles, and 10 (11, 12) sts on second and fourth needles. Work decrease rnd every other rnd as for toe 4 (5, 6) times total–22 sts. Slip sts from second needle onto first needle, and slip sts from fourth needle onto third needle–11 sts each on 2 needles. Use Kitchener stitch to graft remaining sts together. Weave in ends. Make second sock same as first.

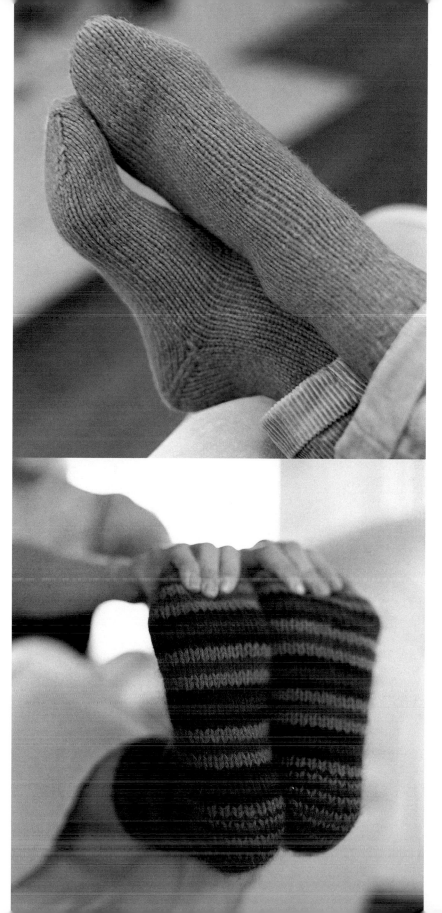

A GOOD READ: KNITTING IN *Literature*

Sometimes it's a toss up. You've got some free time and you want to curl up on the couch, but do you want to knit or do you want to read? For those days when reading wins out, but just barely, here's a list of books I've read with knitting characters. For a much lengthier list, go online and visit www.woolworks.org (click on Resources, then Books That Mention Knitting). As in the list of movies with knitting scenes (see page 22), in some cases knitting plays a significant role in these stories; in others, it's only mentioned briefly.

Adult

Wuthering Heights by Emily Brontë (1847)
In this 19th-century classic, narrator Nelly Dean knits while recounting the tortured history of Wuthering Heights and the poisonous love shared by the two main characters, Catherine and Heathcliff.

A Tale of Two Cities by Charles Dickens (1859)
Madame Defarge, who recorded the crimes of the aristocrats in her knitting at the dawn of the French Revolution, may well be the most famous knitter in literary history. In the chapter called "Still Knitting" she and her followers are described as knitting incessantly to still the pangs of hunger. The chapter ends with this passage: "So much was closing in about the women who sat knitting, knitting, that they their very selves were closing in around a structure yet unbuilt, where they were to sit knitting, knitting, counting dropped heads."

Great Expectations by Charles Dickens (1861)
The unmoved Estella knits continuously even as Pip, an idealistic orphan, declares his enduring love for her in this Dickens classic about the confusion and disappointment that expectations can foster.

Roman Fever and Other Stories by Edith Wharton (1911)
In *Roman Fever*, one of eight stories in this volume, two old friends revisit the past in a conversation that seems to begin innocently (with one woman knitting) but quickly intensifies as an old romantic rivalry resurfaces and new details are revealed.

To the Lighthouse by Virginia Woolf (1927)
When main character Mrs. Ramsay knits, she sinks into herself and feels grounded in this novel about the Ramsay family and the subjective reality of everyday life, especially the male and female experience.

Reasons to Live by Amy Hempel (1985)
In *Beg, Sl Tog, Inc, Cont, Rep*, one of 15 short stories in this volume, a woman compulsively knits for a friend's baby after aborting her own.

The Rat by Günter Grass (1986)
The narrator of this intricately constructed, apocalyptic novel receives as a present a female rat who sets out to prove that rats will inherit a devastated earth. One of the many stories within a story that make up this philosophical tale concerns a group of militant women working on a research barge in the Baltic Sea who knit during every spare moment. The first chapter ends with the narrator speaking to the rat: "Now, She-rat, that forests and rivers, plains and mountains, manifestos and prayers, even banners and leaflets, not to mention heads emptied by speculation, provide indication that our yarn may be running out; now that the end is being postponed from day to day, knitting women are the last counterforce, whereas men just talk everything to pieces and finish nothing, not even mittens capable of supplying warmth to freezing humanity." The author won the 1999 Nobel Prize for Literature.

The Shipping News by E. Annie Proulx (1993)
The knitting traditions of the Newfoundland coast are acknowledged in this Pulitzer Prize-winning novel mostly set there. Among the knitting characters in this story of pain and renewal are a four-year-old girl, a newspaperman, and a trucker who knits while he drives.

Mister Sandman by Barbara Gowdy (1996)
One of three daughters in the eccentric Canary family uses her lightning-fast fingers to package bobby pins and knit hats and scarves for handsome profit.

Children's Picture Books

Goodnight Moon by Margaret Wise Brown (1947)
A quiet bunny rabbit knits in her rocking chair in this classic bedtime tale.

The Lorax by Dr. Seuss (1971)
Knitting takes on a sinister role in Seuss's rhyming story about the dangers of mistreating the environment for personal gain.

The Mitten by Jan Brett (1989)
A beautifully illustrated Ukrainian folktale about a boy who begs his grandmother to knit him white mittens. When he promptly loses one in the snow, a series of animals, including a hedgehog and a bear, snuggle inside of it.

A Symphony for the Sheep by C.M. Millen (1996)
A poetic, beautifully illustrated ode to the sheep of Ireland and the spinning, knitting, and weaving of their wool.

Children's Novels

Little Women by Louisa May Alcott (1869)
Knitting is part of everyday life in this classic, heartwarming story of four spirited sisters growing up in New England during the Civil War.

Through the Looking Glass by Lewis Carroll (1871)
Alice meets a sheep knitting in a shop in this fantastical follow-up to *Alice's Adventures in Wonderland*.

Safe Return by Catherine Dexter (1996)
An 11-year-old girl on a remote Swedish island in the early 1900s knits to calm her fears as she awaits the return of her aunt, who has traveled to Stockholm to sell sweaters knitted by the islanders.

The Harry Potter Series by J.K. Rowling (1998 – present)
Mrs. Weasley, a witch; Hagrid, a warm-hearted giant; and Dobby, an elf, are all knitters in this imaginative series of novels about wizard-in-training Harry Potter.

petticoat socks

VÉRONIK AVERY

An illustration of a petticoat with a scalloped hem in a late-19th-century knitting book inspired Véronik Avery to design these feminine socks. The diagonal stitch-patterning is pretty and unusual and holds the socks in place just as well as the more typical vertical ribbing. Véronik has included directions for working these socks in the round using either five double-pointed needles or two circular needles.

Review notes on page 120 before beginning to knit.

HEMMED TOP EDGE

Using Two Circular Needles

Using one larger and one smaller circ needle held together, CO by wrapping yarn around both needles 52 times. Slide the smaller needle further into the sts so that the CO loops are resting on the cable section of the needle. Using the second larger circ needle, knit across all CO loops. There will be 52 sts on one larger needle, and the smaller needle will hanging from the bottom of the work, through the base of the CO loops. Arrange sts as follows: Slip 26 sts from larger needle to second larger needle. Slip 26 CO loops from smaller needle to second smaller needle. There are now 4 circ needles in the work: 26 live sts each on the two larger needles, and 26 CO loops each on the two smaller needles. Place a removable stitch marker in the work

Finished Sizes
To fit up to woman's US shoe sizes 7 – 8½, approximately 7" circumference, and 9½" long. Leg approximately 8" high (short grape version), or 11" high (long willow version) from floor to top of leg. Notes for customizing the foot length to accommodate a different size foot are given in the pattern.

Yarn
Louet Sales Gems Merino Sport Weight (100% Merino wool; 225 yards / 100 grams): 3 skeins. Shown in #52 grape (purple) and #44 willow (green).

Needles
Two 20" circular (circ) needles size US 2 (2.75 mm).
Two 20" circ needles size US 1 (2.25 mm) or smaller, or one set of 5 double-pointed needles (dpn) size US 2 (2.75 mm).
Change needle size if necessary to obtain the correct gauge.

Notions
Removable stitch marker, yarn needle, small amount of smooth waste yarn (optional).

Gauge
Using larger needles, 26 sts and 40 rounds = 4" in Stockinette stitch (St st) in the round.

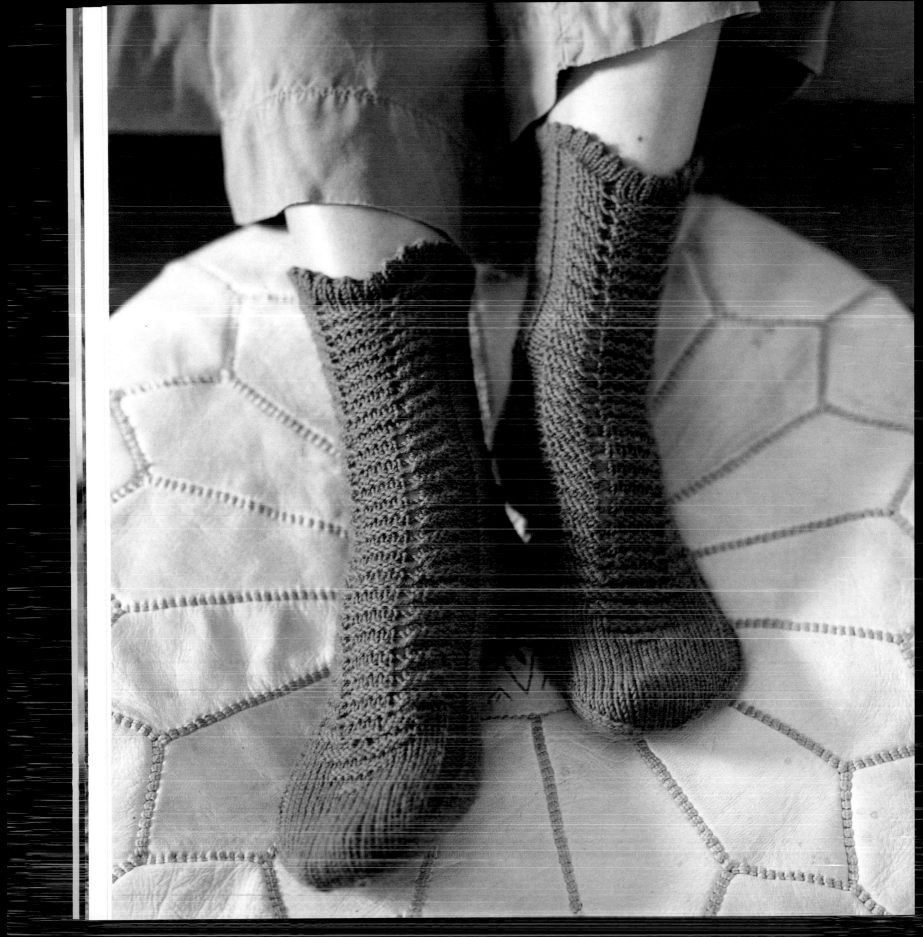

uptown scarf

LINDA NIEMEYER

Here's a great project for a beginning knitter—or any knitter needing a quick fix. The alpaca-merino yarn is soft and luxurious, a treat for the fingers. The color is soothing and beautiful, candy for the eyes. The knitting—garter stitch all the way through—is done on huge needles (size 35), thus gratification is super-quick. Shown here at a dramatic 8 feet, this scarf can be equally appealing at nearly any length.

Sunshine ran to Quoyle, put her
mouth to his ear and sent a
loud, tickling message in.

"Dad, Beety is showing me how
to knit. I am knitting
a Christmas present for you.
It's very hard."

"Good lord," said Quoyle
astonished. "And you're only
four years old."

"It's kind of a trick,
Dad, because it's just a long,
long, fat string and
it turns into a scarf . . . ."

From *The Shipping News*,
E. ANNIE PROULX, 1993

Finished Measurements
3" wide by 96" long, not including fringe.

Yarn
Scarf: Blue Sky Bulky (50% alpaca, 50% wool; 45 yards / 100 grams): 2 skeins.
Fringe: Blue Sky Worsted Hand-Dyes (50% alpaca, 50% wool; 100 yards / 100 grams): approximately 30 yards.
Shown in #1012 blue bulky and #2001 dungaree blue worsted.

Needles
One set straight needles size US 35 (19 mm).
Change needle size if necessary to obtain the correct gauge.

Notions
Yarn needle, crochet hook size S (19 mm) for applying fringe.

Gauge
5 sts and 8 rows = 3" in garter stitch.

SCARF

CO 5 stitches. Work in garter stitch (knit all sts every row) until scarf is 96" (8 feet) long or desired length. With yarn needle, weave in ends.

FRINGE

Cut sixty 18" strands of fringe yarn. For each fringe bundle, take six strands held together and fold them in half. Use crochet hook to draw the folded loop through one end st of scarf. Draw the loose ends through the loop and pull snugly. Apply five fringe bundles to each end of scarf. Trim ends neatly.

charm of children

luggy bonnet

LUCY MACKENZIE & KIRSTEEN MITCALFE

One of these adorable Luggy Bonnets from Pride and Joy, a British children's knitwear company, was *almost* worn by Harry Potter in the film adaptation of J. K. Rowling's *Harry Potter and the Sorcerer's Stone*. A bonnet with stars was requested for the scene when baby Harry is left at the doorstep of his evil Aunt Petunia and Uncle Vernon. But it was never used, according to the costume designer, because the weather was warm and the baby didn't need it. Pride and Joy didn't completely miss its shot at Harry Potter magic, however: Ron Weasley's *R* sweater, worn on Christmas morning, is a Pride and Joy creation.

When **the** photographer for *Weekend Knitting*, Ericka McConnell, saw the heart Luggy Bonnet shown here, she immediately exclaimed, "I want one in my size." So, with the designers' permission, adult sizing was added to the pattern.

EAR FLAPS (make 2)

Using MC, CO 6 sts and purl 1 row. Beginning with a knit row, work St st, changing colors every 2 rows for random stripes of your choice (see below for stripe sequences of hats pictured), and, at the same time, inc 1 st at each end of needle every row 4 times, then every other row 3 (4, 5, 6) times—20 (22, 24, 26) sts. After shaping has been completed, continue even in 2-row stripes until 22 (24, 26, 28) rows have been worked after the beginning purl row. Place sts on holder. Make

Finished Sizes
To fit 6 to 18 months (18 months to 4 years, 4 years to adult small, adult medium to large).

Finished Measurements
Approximately 17½ (20, 21, 23)" around. Shown in size 17½" with yellow hearts, and in size 20" with blue stars.

Yarn
Jaeger Matchmaker Merino DK or Baby Merino (100% machine-washable Merino wool; 130 yards / 50 grams): 1 skein each main color (MC) and 8 accent colors. Yarn used in sample hats shown is Merino DK unless Baby Merino is specified.
Yellow heart hat shown in #219 cranberry Baby Merino (MC), #862 butter (yellow), #867 dill (green), #870 rosy, #882 haze (lilac), #877 gold, #662 cream, #875 Victoria (deep purple), and #866 Airforce (slate blue).
Blue star hat shown in #629 mariner (medium blue, MC), with #862 butter (yellow), #868 raspberry, #856 buddleia (purple), #219 cranberry Baby Merino, #662 cream, #869 rain (light blue), #890 seaweed (olive), #655 burgundy.

Needles
One set straight needles size US 6 (4 mm).
Change needle size if necessary to obtain the correct gauge.

Notions
Stitch holders, stitch markers, yarn needle, size F (4 mm) crochet hook.

Gauge
22 sts and 33 rows = 4" in Stockinette stitch (St st).

"I think I know who that one's from," said Ron, turning a bit pink and pointing to a very lumpy parcel. "My mum. I told her you didn't expect any presents and— oh, no," he groaned, "she's made you a Weasley sweater."

Harry had torn open the parcel to find a thick, hand-knitted sweater in emerald green and a large box of homemade fudge.

"Every year she makes us a sweater," said Ron, unwrapping his own, "and mine's always maroon."

"That's really nice of her," said Harry, trying the fudge, which was very tasty.

From *Harry Potter and the Sorcerer's Stone*,
J. K. ROWLING, 1999

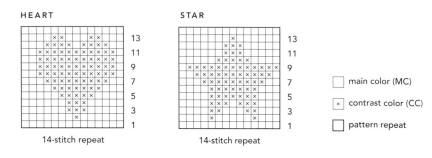

HEART   **STAR**

□ main color (MC)
× contrast color (CC)
□ pattern repeat

14-stitch repeat   14-stitch repeat

Work RS (odd-numbered) rows from right to left, and work WS (un-numbered) rows from left to right.

second ear flap same as the first and place on holder.

Stripe sequence shown for yellow heart hat earflaps: 2 rows each *cranberry, yellow, green, rosy, lilac, gold, cream, deep purple, slate blue; repeat from * for the number of rows required for your size.

Stripe sequence shown for blue star hat earflaps: 2 rows each *medium blue, yellow, raspberry, purple, cranberry, cream, light blue, olive, burgundy; repeat from * for the number of rows required for your size.

LOWER HAT
Using MC, CO 13 (15, 16, 17) sts. Knit across these 13 (15, 16, 17) sts, with first flap held RS facing you knit across 20 (22, 24, 26) sts of first ear flap, CO 31 (36, 36, 41) sts, knit across 20 (22, 24, 26) sts of second ear flap, CO 13 (15, 16, 17) sts—97 (110, 116, 127) sts. Purl 1 row with MC. Change to another color and work 14 (18, 20, 24) rows in random 2-color stripes of your choice (see below for stripe sequences of hats pictured).

Stripe sequence shown for body of yellow heart hat: after working 2 rows in burgundy to join the ear flaps, work 2 rows each *green, rosy, lilac, gold, cream, deep purple, slate blue; repeat from * for the number of rows required for your size.

Stripe sequence shown for body of blue star hat: after working 2 rows medium blue to join the earflaps, work 2 rows each *purple, cranberry, cream, light blue, olive, burgundy, medium blue, yellow; repeat from * for the number of rows required for your size.

MOTIF BAND

With MC as the background, and using the CC color of your choice, work one of the charts on page 136, setting up chart as given below. Colors used for hats shown: yellow hearts (CC) on cranberry (MC) background, or light blue stars (CC) on medium blue (MC) background.

Heart or Star Chart: Work 7 (6, 2, 1) sts MC, pm (place marker), work 14-stitch chart repeat 6 (7, 8, 9) times, pm, work 6 (6, 2, 0) sts MC. Continue as established, working sts outside the markers in MC only, until Row 14 of chart has been completed.

SHAPE TOP

Change to 2-row random stripes of your choice, and work 0 (2, 4, 6) rows even. Continuing 2-row stripes, shape top as follows (see below for stripe sequences of hats pictured):

ROW 1: (RS) [K2, k2tog, k3, k2tog] 10 (11, 12, 13) times, k2, k2tog, k3 (7, 4, 6)—76 (87, 91, 100) sts.

ROWS 2–10: Work even.

ROW 11: K1, [k2tog, k1] 25 (28, 30, 33) times, k0 (k2tog, k0, k0)—51 (58, 61, 67) sts.

ROWS 12–14: Work even.

ROW 15: K1, k2tog 25 (28, 29, 33) times, k0 (1, 2, 0)—26 (30, 32, 34) sts.

ROW 16: Work 1 row even to complete stripe in progress. For smallest size *only*, skip to Row 19.

ROWS 17–18: Work even.

ROWS 19–22: Change to MC and work 4 rows.

ROW 23: K2tog around—13 (15, 16, 17) sts remain.

ROWS 24–26: Work 3 rows in MC.

ROW 25: K1 (1, 0, 1) [k2tog] 6 (7, 8, 8) times—7 (8, 8, 9) sts.

Stripe sequence shown for top of yellow heart hat: slate blue, deep purple, cream, gold, lilac, rosy, green, yellow, then shape top using cranberry to ends.

Stripe sequence shown for top of blue star hat: yellow, medium blue, burgundy, olive, light blue, cream, cranberry, purple, raspberry, yellow, then shape top using medium blue to end.

Break yarn, leaving an 8" tail. Thread tail through remaining sts and pull tightly. Weave in ends.

FINISHING

Sew back seam. With RS facing, using MC, work 1 row of double crochet (see Notes) around bottom edge, working 2 double crochets at the bottom corners of each flap to turn the corners. Join last loop on hook to first double crochet using a slipstitch (see Notes). Do not turn. Work 1 row of reverse double crochet (from left to right; see Notes) around bottom edge, working 2 reverse double crochets together at each corner where the flaps meet the main body of the hat. Fasten off. Block hat lightly, if desired.

curly-toed elf slippers

slippers

KATE SOKOLOFF

Inspired by the children's classic *The Elves and the Shoemaker* by the Brothers Grimm, Kate Sokoloff designed these whimsical slippers with bulky quick-knit yarn so, she says, "they can magically appear overnight to warm the elf-toes of children." *Weekend Knitting* technical editor Lori Gayle came up with the idea to adapt the pattern to include the Christmas stocking on page 140.

Review notes on page 141 before beginning to knit.

LEG

With larger dpn and bootie yarn, CO 14 (16, 18) [32] sts. Place marker and join, being careful not to twist. Work garter stitch in the round (purl one rnd, knit one rnd) for 15 (17, 19) [47] rnds, beginning and ending with a purl rnd. Piece measures approximately 4 (4½, 5)" [12"], including CO. Rearrange sts, if necessary, so there are 7 (8, 9) [16] sts on the first needle, 3 (4, 5) [8] sts on the second needle, and 4 (4, 4) [8] sts on the third needle.

HEEL

Heel is worked back and forth in garter stitch (knit every row) on the 7 (8, 9) [16] sts of the first needle. Work short rows to shape heel as follows:
ROW 1: (RS) Sl (slip) 1 yb (with yarn in back), k5 (6, 7) [14], wrap and turn (see Notes).

Finished Sizes
To fit up to child's shoe size 4 (7, 11½). Christmas stocking approximately 14" around the top opening, and 18" long from top to toe.

Yarn
Booties: *Version 1:* GGH Fantastica, (70% wool, 10% alpaca, 15% acrylic, 5% nylon; 30 yards / 50 grams): 2 (2, 3) balls for children's sizes, 5 balls for Christmas stocking. *Version 2:* GGH Horstia Marokko, (100% wool; 87 yards / 200 grams): 1 skein for all children's sizes, 2 skeins for Christmas stocking. *Version 3:* GGH Naturwolle, (100% wool; 110 yards / 100 grams): 2 skeins for all children's sizes, 3 skeins for Christmas stocking (used doubled throughout). **Cuffs:** GGH Apart (100% nylon; 121 yards / 50 grams): 1 ball for all versions (used doubled throughout).

Slippers shown on page 139 (left to right) in Fantastica #4 orange mix with Apart #11 orange; in Fantastica #7 blue-green with Apart #16 fuchsia; and Marokko #111 blue with Apart #15 teal. Christmas stocking on page 140 shown in Naturwolle #soft 02 variegated orange with Apart #16 fuchsia.

Needles
One set of four double-pointed needles (dpn) size US 9 (5.5 mm).
One set of four dpn size US 13 (9 mm). The stocking may also be knitted on a short circular needle, changing to dpn when necessary. Change needle size if necessary to obtain the correct gauge.

Notions
Stitch marker, yarn needle, 6" length of shoelace for reinforcing hanging loop (optional, for Christmas stocking).

Gauge
Using slipper yarn and larger needles, 7 sts = 3", and 16 rounds = 4" in garter st in the round.

ROW 2: K5 (6, 7) [14], wrap and turn. There is now 1 wrapped st at each side of heel.

ROW 3: K4 (5, 6) [13], wrap and turn.

ROW 4: K3 (4, 5) [12], wrap and turn. There are now 2 wrapped sts at each side of heel.

ROW 5: K2 (3, 4) [11], wrap and turn.

ROW 6: K1 (2, 3) [10] wrap and turn. There are now 3 wrapped sts at each side of heel.

For the two smallest children's sizes, skip to *For all sizes* at right.

For largest child's size and Christmas stocking only

ROW 7: K2 [9], wrap and turn.

ROW 8: K1 [8], wrap and turn. There are now 4 wrapped sts at each side of heel for largest child's size and the Christmas stocking. For the largest child's size, skip to *For all sizes* below.

For Christmas stocking only

ROW 9: K7, wrap and turn.

ROW 10: K6, wrap and turn. There are now 5 wrapped sts at each side of heel.

ROW 11: K5, wrap and turn.

ROW 12: K4, wrap and turn. There are now 6 wrapped sts at each side of heel.

For all sizes

ROW 1: (RS) Sl 1 yb, k0 (1, 0) [3], with point of right-hand needle lift the wrap at the base of the next st onto the left-hand needle and k2tog tbl (the wrap and the stitch together; see Notes), turn.

ROW 2: Sl 1 yf (with yarn in front), k1 (2, 1) [4], lift wrap at base of next st and k2tog tbl, turn.

ROW 3: Sl 1 yb, k2 (3, 2) [5], lift wrap at base of next st and k2tog tbl, turn.

ROW 4: Sl 1 yf, k3 (4, 3) [6], lift wrap at base of next st and k2tog tbl, turn.

ROW 5: Sl 1 yb, k4 (5, 4) [7], lift wrap at base of next st and k2tog tbl, turn.

ROW 6: Sl 1 yf, k5 (6, 5) [8], lift wrap at base of next st and k2tog tbl, turn. For the two smallest children's sizes, skip to *For all sizes* below.

For largest child's size and Christmas stocking only

ROW 7: Sl 1 yb, k6 [9], lift wrap at base of next st and k2tog tbl, turn.

ROW 8: Sl 1 yf, k7 [10], lift wrap at base of next st and k2tog tbl, turn. For the largest children's size, skip to *For all sizes* at right.

Every child is an artist.
The problem is
how to remain an artist
once he grows up.

PABLO PICASSO

notes

- Instructions for children's sizes are given first; instructions for Christmas stocking follow in [ ].

- All slipped stitches are slipped as if to purl, unless otherwise noted.

- **Wrap and Turn:** Bring yarn to front of work, slip the next st to right-hand needle, bring yarn to back of work, return first st on right-hand needle to left-hand needle, and turn work, ready to work the next row.

- To work a wrap together with its wrapped stitch, insert the tip of the right-hand needle under the wrap, from front to back, and lift the wrap onto the left-hand needle. If necessary, use the tip of the right-hand needle to pry open the wrap and its stitch slightly to make it easier to knit both together through the back of their loops.

- **K2tog tbl:** Knit 2 together through the back of their loops, twisting the stitches.

- **Ssk (slip, slip, knit):** Slip next 2 sts to right-hand needle one at a time as if to knit, pass them back to left-hand needle one at a time in their new orientation, knit them together through back of their loops.

- **Ssp (slip, slip, purl):** Slip 2 sts to right-hand needle one at a time as if to knit, pass them back to left-hand needle one at a time in their new orientation, and purl them together through the back of their loops.

- **I-Cord:** On one double-pointed needle, cast on or pick up the required number of sts. *Transfer the needle with the sts to your left hand, with the working yarn hanging down from the last (bottom) stitch on the needle. Bring the yarn around behind the work and knit the sts in the same order again (so working yarn is pulled up from the bottom stitch to the top stitch when you start a new row); repeat from * until the cord is the length desired.

- **Kitchener Stitch:** On a yarn needle, thread a length of yarn approximately 4 times the length of the section to be grafted closed. Hold needles with sts to be grafted with wrong sides of work together. Working from right to left, *insert yarn needle in first stitch on front dpn as if to knit, pull yarn through, remove st from dpn. Insert yarn needle into next st on front dpn as if to purl, pull yarn through, leave st on dpn. Insert yarn needle into first st on back dpn as if to purl, pull yarn through, remove st from dpn. Insert yarn needle into next st on back dpn as if to knit, pull yarn through, leave st on dpn. Repeat from * until 1 st remains on each dpn. Cut yarn and pass through last 2 sts to fasten off.

For Christmas stocking only

ROW 9: K11, lift wrap at base of next st and k2tog tbl, turn.
ROW 10: K12, lift wrap at base of next st and k2tog tbl, turn.
ROW 11: K13, lift wrap at base of next st and k2tog tbl, turn.
ROW 12: K14, lift wrap at base of next st and k2tog tbl, turn.

For all sizes

Knit one rnd on all sts, closing gaps at heel corners as follows: *Insert the left needle tip from below into the purl loop 2 rnds below the last st of the previous rnd, scoop up the purl loop, and place it on the left needle, k2tog (the first st of the rnd and the picked up purl loop), k6 (7, 8) [15] to end of first needle; with point of second needle, in the same manner scoop up the purl loop below the last stitch on the first needle and k2tog (the first st of the second needle and the picked up loop), knit to end of rnd—14 (16, 18) [32] sts; 7 (8, 9) [16] sts on first needle, 3 (4, 5) [8] sts on the second needle, and 4 (4, 4) [8] sts on the third needle.

FOOT

Work in garter stitch in the rnd for 7 (11, 13) [17] rnds, beginning and ending with a purl rnd.

SHAPE TOE

RND 1: Ssk (see Notes), knit to last 2 sts of first needle, k2tog, knit to end of rnd—12 (14, 16) [30] sts.
RND 2: Purl all sts on first needle, ssp first 2 sts of next needle (see Notes), purl to last 2 sts of rnd, p2tog—10 (12, 14) [28] sts.
Repeat Rnds 1 and 2 once more—6 (8, 10) [24] sts.

For largest size only
Work Rnd 1 once more, then purl one rnd without shaping—8 sts.

For Christmas stocking only
Repeat Rnds 1 and 2 three more times—12 sts.

For all sizes
6 (8, 8) [12] sts remain after toe shaping. Cut yarn, leaving a 12" tail. Arrange sts on 2 needles: 3 (4, 4) [6] sts on needle for sole of the foot, and 3 (4, 4) [6] sts on needle for instep. Use Kitchener stitch (see Notes) to graft toe closed.

TOE CURL
Using smaller dpn and RS facing, using slipper yarn, pick up and knit 3 [4] sts on the instep side of the foot, picking up in the purl loops of the rnd just below the grafting by inserting the needle into them from below, and scooping up the loops onto the needle. Turn work, and with a second dpn, pick up 3 [4] sts from the base of the sts on the first needle in the same manner—6 [8] sts. Working in the round, knit 3 rnds. Next rnd: *Sl 1 as if to knit yb, k1, pass slipped st over, k1 [2]; repeat from * once—4 [6] sts. Knit 3 rnds.

For Christmas stocking only
Next rnd: *K1, k2tog; repeat from * once (4 sts remain), then knit 3 rnds on all sts.

For all sizes
Next rnd: K2tog twice—2 sts. Slip both sts to one needle and work I-cord for 3 rows. Next row: K2tog—1 st. *Knit the single st, pass it back to left needle; repeat from * 7 more times. Cut yarn and fasten off last st. Weave in the yarn end, and pull snugly to coax the tip of the curl into a curve before securing the end. With another strand of yarn, fasten curl to top of foot as shown in photograph.

CUFF
With smaller dpn and RS facing, using a doubled strand of cuff yarn, pick up and knit 1 st in each CO st around leg opening—14 (16, 18) [32] sts. Join, and place marker for beginning of rnd. Next rnd: *K1, make 1 st by knitting into the strand between the needles; repeat from * to end—28 (32, 36) [64] sts. Knit every rnd until cuff measures 2½ (3, 3½)" [5"]. BO all sts very loosely. Make second slipper same as first.

FINISHING
Weave in all ends. Fold cuff down; the fluffier purl side will be facing outward. For Chrismas stocking, make a hanging loop from a 6" length of 3-st I-cord, using "slipper" yarn and smaller needles and working firmly. To prevent I-cord from stretching, run a length of shoelace up the center of the cord. Sew securely to stocking as shown.

"Then I hope your finger is better now," Alice said very politely, as she crossed the little brook after the Queen.

'Oh, much better!' cried the Queen, her voice rising into a squeak as she went on. 'Much be-etter! Be-etter! Be-e-e-etter! Be-e-ehh!' The last word ended in a long bleat, so like a sheep that Alice quite started.

She looked at the Queen, who seemed to have suddenly wrapped herself up in wool. Alice rubbed her eyes, and looked again. She couldn't make out what had happened at all. Was she in a shop? And was that really—was it really a *sheep* that was sitting on the other side of the counter? Rub as she would, she could making nothing more of it: she was in a little dark shop, and leaning with her elbows on the counter, and opposite to her was an old Sheep, sitting in an arm-chair knitting, and every now and then leaving off to look at her through a great pair of spectacles.

From *Through the Looking Glass,*
LEWIS CARROLL, 1872

pig-tailed dolly

JO SHARP

This heirloom blanket is sized for a stroller, car seat, or other place where baby needs to be kept warm. The classic plaid looks especially fresh in the unisex yellow, blue, and lime palette. The lining is solid-color Stockinette stitch, which—depending on your mood—could be relaxing or, let's face it, tedious to knit. If you'd prefer not to knit the lining, buy 3 skeins fewer putty-colored yarn and follow the instructions for sewing on a fabric backing. The accompanying dolly can be completed in a few hours—and enjoyed for years. Her pants are "built in," but her heart sweater can be taken on and off.

Review notes on page 146 before beginning to knit.

Baby Blanket

FRONT

Using larger needles and putty, CO 134 sts. Work from blanket chart on page 148, working each vertical stripe of the plaid with a separate length of yarn (intarsia-style, twisting yarns at color changes to avoid leaving holes), and working background in bands of putty, natural, or stranded colorwork Stockinette stitch (St st) as shown. Beginning with Row 1 (RS), work the 24-st repeat five times, then work the sts outside the repeat box once. Work Rows 1 to 44 four times—176 rows total. BO all sts.

KNITTED LINING

Using larger needles and putty, CO 134 sts. Work 3 rows St st, beginning

Finished Measurements
Baby blanket: Approximately 27" long and 24" wide.
Doll: 11" tall.

Yarn
Jo Sharp Soho Summer DK (100% cotton; 109 yards / 50 grams).
Doll: 1 skein each #227 putty, #221 Carmen (red), #228 calico (natural), #226 umber (brown).
Blanket: 6 skeins #227 putty; 3 skeins #228 calico (natural); 1 skein each #222 freesia (yellow), #218 cloudless (light blue), and #223 cactus (lime green).

Needles
One set straight needles size US 3 (3.25 mm).
One set straight needles size US 6 (4 mm).
Change needle size if necessary to obtain the correct gauge.

Notions
Yarn needle, stitch holders, polyester fiberfill for stuffing doll, crochet hook size H (5 mm) or larger for blanket fringe, ¾ yard 45" cotton fabric for blanket lining (optional).

Gauge
For blanket, using larger needles, 22 sts and 30 rows = 4" in Stockinette St.
For doll, using smaller needles, 24 sts and 36 rows = 4" in St st.

- **M1 (make 1):** Insert tip of left-hand needle under the strand between the two needles, from back to front, and lift this strand onto the left-hand needle. Knit the lifted strand through the front loop to increase 1 st.

- **Ssk (slip, slip, knit):** Slip the next 2 sts to right-hand needle one at a time as if to knit, pass these 2 sts back to the left-hand needle one at a time in their new orientation and knit them together through the back of their loops.

- **Ssp (slip, slip, purl):** Slip the next 2 sts to right-hand needle one at a time as if to knit, pass these 2 sts back to the left-hand needle one at a time in their new orientation and purl them together through the back of their loops.

- **Pf&b (purl front and back):** Purl the next st through the front of its loop, then through the back of its loop, to increase 1 st.

and ending with a purl row. Change to yellow and work 3 rows St st, beginning and ending with a knit row. Change to putty and work even in St st until piece measures 3½" from beginning, ending with a WS row. Next row: (RS) Purl all sts to create a fold line. Resume working in St st until piece measures 27" from fold line, or 30½" from beginning. BO all sts.

FINISHING

Press pieces gently on WS using a warm iron over a damp cloth. Sew front and lining together along bottom and sides. Fold lining along fold line and sew sides of lining extension. The blanket will still be open along the top edge of front. Using 2 strands each of yellow, blue, and green, make a braid the width of the blanket. Center the braid on the lining's 3-row stripe of yellow and sew in place.

Close the front opening using sections of putty fringe as follows. For each fringe section, cut 4 strands 4" long and fold in half. Position blanket with WS of lining and front held together, edges of the opening aligned, and the front of blanket facing you. Beginning at side of blanket, insert crochet hook through both the front and lining as close to the edge as possible and catch the folded strands. Pull up a loop, insert the loose ends of the strands through the loop, and pull gently to tighten. Leaving a 1-st space between each fringe section, continue across the opening until it has been completely closed by fringe. Trim ends even.

For optional purchased fabric lining, cut a piece 31½" long and 25½" wide. Turn under ½" around all edges and press. Fold one short side down another 3½" and press. Sew

front and lining together along bottom and sides. Sew sides of 3½" lining extension closed. The blanket will still be open along the top edge of front. Attach putty fringe as given above for knitted lining, except each fringe section should be hooked through the front of the blanket only (do not hook fringe through purchased fabric). When fringe has been completed, sew lining to front along top edge. If desired, trim with 3-color braid as given for knitted lining as follows: Using 2 strands each of yellow, blue, and green, make a braid the width of the blanket. Position the braid ½" from the front edge of the lining extension. Sew braid in place.

Doll

LEGS (make 2)

Using putty and smaller needles, CO 10 sts.

ROW 1: (RS) Knit.

ROWS 2, 4, 6, AND 8: Purl.

ROW 3: K1, M1 (see Notes), knit to last 2 sts, M1, k2—12 sts.

ROW 5: Repeat Row 3—14 sts.

ROW 7: Repeat Row 3—16 sts.

ROW 9: Repeat Row 3—18 sts.

ROW 10: Purl.

Change to red and natural. Continuing in St st, *work 2 rows red, then 2 rows natural; repeat from * 8 more times—36 rows of stripes completed. Place sts on holder and complete second leg same as the first.

BODY

Transfer sts on holders for legs to a single needle and join red yarn ready to work a RS row—36 sts. Work 14 rows St st. Change to putty and work 10 rows St st. BO all sts.

ARMS (make 2)

Using putty and smaller needles, CO 8 sts.

ROW 1: (RS) Knit.

ROWS 2 AND 4: Purl.

ROW 3: K1, M1, knit to last 2 sts, M1, k2—10 sts.

ROW 5: Repeat Row 3—12 sts.

ROW 6: Purl.

Work 36 more rows St st. BO all sts. Make a second arm the same as the first. Sew arm seams, stuff arms, and sew tops of arms closed.

HEAD (make 2)

The head is made in front and back halves, worked from the neck to the top of the head.

Using putty and smaller needles, CO 12 sts.

ROW 1: (RS) Knit.

ROW 2: Purl.

ROW 3: K1, ssk (see Notes), knit to last 3 sts, k2tog, k1—10 sts.

ROW 4: P1, ssp (see Notes), purl to last 3 sts, p2tog, p1—8 sts.

ROW 5: Knit.

ROW 6: P1, pf&b (see Notes), purl to last 2 sts, pf&b, p1—10 sts.

ROW 7: K1, M1, knit to last st, M1, k1—12 sts.

ROWS 8 AND 10: Purl.

ROW 9: Repeat Row 7—14 sts.

ROW 11: Repeat Row 7—16 sts.

ROWS 12–18: Work in St st.

ROW 19: Repeat Row 3—14 sts.

ROWS 20 AND 22: Purl.

ROW 21: Repeat Row 3—12 sts.

ROW 23: Repeat Row 3—10 sts.

ROW 24: Repeat Row 4—8 sts.

ROW 25: Repeat Row 3—6 sts.

ROW 26: P2tog 3 times—3 sts.

BO all sts.

Using brown, make a second head piece like the first one.

pullover & cardigan

LANA HAMES

This fun-to-knit baby sweater boasts a sophisticated simplicity that suits babies perfectly. Made with hemp yarn, which comes from an ecofriendly plant of the same name, it is soft (and gets softer with each washing) yet durable (hemp is the longest fiber in the world, which makes it very strong). The construction of the sweater, mainly in garter stitch, is unusual, but not at all difficult. The body pieces are knitted separately, from side to side (rather than the more traditional bottom to top), which means the garter ridges run vertically instead of horizontally. The sleeves are started at the underarm with stitches quickly added from the armhole to the wrist and knitted back and forth around the arm rather than from cuff to shoulder (again bucking tradition), so that the garter ridges run vertically here as well. The buttons are made from corozo nut, a natural product of a South American palm tree.

Review notes on page 152 before beginning to knit.

Cardigan

BACK

Using larger needle, CO 27 (31, 34, 37) sts, then using smaller needle, CO 4 (4, 5, 5) sts—31 (35, 39, 42) sts.

ROW 1: (WS) Using smaller needle, k4 (4, 5, 5) sts, using larger needle, k27 (31, 34, 37) sts.

ROW 2: (RS) With larger needle, k27 (31, 34, 37) sts, using smaller needle, p4 (4, 5, 5).

ROW 3: Repeat Row 1.

Finished Sizes
To fit 0 – 6 months (6 – 9 months, 9 – 12 months, 12 – 18 months).

Finished Measurements
20 (22, 24, 26)" chest

Yarn
Cardigan: Hemp for Knitting™ All Hemp, Hemp 6 (100% long line, wetspun hemp; 93 yards / 50 grams): 3 (4, 6, 7) balls. Shown in 20" size in natural.
Pullover: Weldon Sisters Changing Colors Naturally, Hemp 6 (100% long line, wetspun; 186 yards/ 100 grams): 2 (2, 3) skeins. Shown in 20" size in madder.

Needles
One 24" circular (circ) needle size US 5 (3.75 mm).
One 24" circular (circ) needle size US 2 (3 mm).
Change needle size if necessary to obtain the correct gauge.

Notions
5 (5, 6, 6) 18-mm corozo nut buttons for cardigan (#SPN 108-18), 4 (4, 4, 5) 24-mm corozo nut buttons for pullover (#SPN 108-24), yarn needle. Buttons shown are from One World Button Supply Co.

Gauge
20 sts and 36 rows = 4" in garter stitch using larger needle.

Sew sleeve caps to armhole edges. Sew sleeve and side seams. Weave in loose ends. Sew on buttons opposite buttonholes. Wash and block sweater to finished measurements.

Pullover

BACK

Work same as cardigan including back neck shaping until piece measures 7 (7½, 8, 8½)" from beginning, ending with a WS row—46 (52, 58, 63) sts. Shoulder button band: At beginning of next RS row, CO 5 sts and work them seed st as follows: (K1, p1) 2 times, k1; then work in patterns as established to end—51 (57, 63, 68) sts. Next row: Work in pattern to last 5 sts, end (k1, p1) 2 times, k1. Repeat the last 2 rows until piece measures 9½ (10½, 11½, 12½)" from beginning, ending with a WS row.

Armhole shaping: At beg of next row, BO 20 (22, 24, 26) sts, work to end—31 (35, 39, 42) sts. Work 4 rows even in patterns. BO all sts loosely.

FRONT

Work first 3 rows same as cardigan back—31 (35, 39, 42) sts. Buttonhole band and armhole shaping: (RS) Using cable cast-on method, CO 16 (18, 20, 22) sts, work to end in patterns as established—47 (53, 59, 64) sts. Work in patterns as established until piece measures 1" from beginning, ending with a WS row. Buttonhole row: (RS) K2, yo (see Notes), k2tog, work in pattern to end. Continue in established patterns until piece measures ¾ (1, 1¼, 1)" from first buttonhole row, ending with a WS row. Work buttonhole row as before. Continue in established patterns until piece measures ¾ (1, 1¼, 1)" from second buttonhole, ending with a WS row. Work buttonhole row as before. For size 12 – 18 months only, work in established patterns until piece measures 1" from third buttonhole, ending with a WS row, then work one more buttonhole row—3 (3, 3, 4) buttonholes completed, piece measures 2½ (3, 3½, 4)" from beginning. Work even until piece measures 3 (3½, 4, 4½)" from beginning, ending with a WS row. Front neck shaping: (RS) BO 7 sts, work to end—40 (46, 52, 57) sts. Work 1 WS row. Next row: BO 1 (2, 3, 4) sts, work to end—39 (44, 49, 53) sts.

Work in patterns as established until piece measures 6½ (7, 7½, 8)" from beginning, ending with a WS row.
ROW 1: (RS) CO 1 (2, 3, 4) sts, work to end—40 (46, 52, 57) sts.
ROW 2: Work even in pattern.
ROW 3: CO 7 sts, work to end—47 (53, 59, 64) sts.

Work in patterns as established until piece measures 9½ (10½, 11½, 12½)" from beginning, ending with a WS row.

Armhole shaping: At beg of next row BO 16 (18, 20, 22) sts, work to end—31 (35, 39, 42) sts. Work 4 rows even. BO all sts loosely.

SLEEVES

Work same as for cardigan.

NECKBAND

Sew front to back at right shoulder. With smaller needle and RS facing, beginning at open left shoulder seam, pick up and knit 40 (42, 46, 46) sts along front neck to shoulder seam, 26 (28, 30, 32) sts across back neck—66 (70, 76, 78) sts. Purl 1 row. Next row: (RS) K2, yo, k2tog, knit to end. Purl 1 row. Knit 2 rows. BO all sts loosely.

FINISHING

Sew sleeve caps to armhole edges. Sew sleeve and side seams. Weave in loose ends. Sew on buttons opposite buttonholes. Wash and block sweater to finished measurements.

I think that learning to knit is so much more valuable to children than being put in front of a computer.

VIVIENNE WESTWOOD

notes

- **M1 (make 1):** Insert tip of left-hand needle under the strand between the two needles, from front to back, and lift this strand onto the left-hand needle. Knit the lifted strand through the back of its loop to increase 1 st.

- **2/2LC (left-crossing cable, worked 2 sts over 2 sts):** Slip the next 2 sts to cable needle (cn) and hold in front, k2, k2 from cn.

- **Seed Stitch (even number of stitches)**
  ROW 1: (RS) *K1, p1; repeat from * to end.
  ROW 2: *P1, k1; repeat from * to end.
  Repeat these 2 rows for pattern.
  To continue seed stitch after shaping, or over an odd number of stitches, knit the purl stitches and purl the knit stitches as they appear.

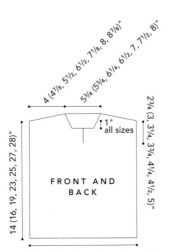

FRONT AND BACK

4 (4⅞, 5½, 6½, 7⅛, 8, 8⅞)"

5¾ (5¾, 6¼, 6½, 7, 7½, 8)"

1" all sizes

2¾ (3, 3¼, 3¾, 4¼, 4½, 5)"

14 (16, 19, 23, 25, 27, 28)"

13¾ (15½, 17¼, 19½, 21¼, 23½, 25¾)"

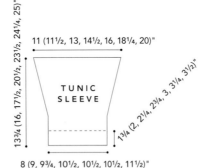

TUNIC SLEEVE

11 (11½, 13, 14½, 16, 18¼, 20)"

13¾ (16, 17½, 20½, 23½, 24¼, 25)"

1¾ (2, 2¼, 2¾, 3, 3¼, 3½)"

8 (9, 9¾, 10½, 10½, 10½, 11½)"

Shape shoulders: BO 13 (15, 18, 20, 22, 24, 27) sts at beg of next 2 rows, working 2 sts together twice (either k2tog or p2tog) at the top of each 4-st cable—52 (56, 62, 68, 76, 82, 90) sts. BO 13 (15, 17, 19, 22, 24, 27) sts at beg of next 2 rows, working 2 sts together twice at the top of each 4-st cable—26 (26, 28, 30, 32, 34, 36) sts remain. Place sts on holder for back neck.

FRONT

Work as for back until front measures 11¼ (13, 15¾, 19¼, 20¾, 22½, 23)" from beginning, ending with a WS row. On next row, establish front neckline slit as follows: (RS) Work in pattern for 39 (43, 49, 54, 60, 65, 72) sts, turn, and work in pattern to end. Working back and forth on these 39 (43, 49, 54, 60, 65, 72) sts only, work even in pattern until front neckline slit measures 1¾ (2, 2¼, 2¾, 3¼, 3½, 4), ending with a WS row. Shape neck: (RS) Work in pattern to last 6 (6, 7, 8, 9, 10, 11) sts, place sts at end of row on a holder, turn—33 (37, 42, 46, 51, 55, 61) sts. Continue in pattern, decreasing 1 st at neck edge every row 7 times—26 (30, 35, 39, 44, 48, 54) sts remain after working 7 neck shaping rows. Work even until piece measures 14 (16, 19, 23, 25, 27, 28)" from beginning, ending with a WS row.

Shape shoulder: Working 2 sts tog at the top of each 4-st cable as for back, BO 13 (15, 18, 20, 22, 24, 27) sts at the beginning of the next RS row, work 1 WS row even, then BO 13 (15, 17, 19, 22, 24, 27) sts at the beginning of the following RS row. With RS facing, rejoin yarn to sts for other side of front—39 (43, 49, 54, 60, 65, 72) sts. Work even in pattern until neckline slit measures 1¾ (2, 2¼, 2¾, 3¼, 3½, 4)", ending with a RS row. Shape neck: (WS) Work in pattern to last 6 (6, 7, 8, 9, 10, 11) sts, place sts at end of row on a holder, turn—33 (37, 42, 46, 51, 55, 61) sts. Continue in pattern, decreasing 1 st at neck edge every row 7 times—26 (30, 35, 39, 44, 48, 54) sts remain after working 7 neck shaping rows. Work even if necessary until piece measures 14 (16, 19, 23, 25, 27, 28)" from beginning, ending with a RS row. Shape shoulder: Working 2 sts tog at the top of each 4-st cable as for back, BO 13 (15, 18, 20, 22, 24, 27) sts at the beginning of the next WS row, work 1 RS row even, then BO 13 (15, 17, 19, 22, 24, 27) sts at the beginning of the following WS row.

NECKBAND
Sew shoulder seams. With smaller needles and RS facing, place 6 (6, 7, 8, 9, 10, 11) sts from right front holder onto needle and work across them in seed st pattern as established, pick up and knit 10 (10, 11, 12, 11, 12, 13) sts along right front neck, place 26 (26, 28, 30, 32, 34, 36) sts from back neck holder on needle and work in seed st, working k2tog twice at the top of each complete 4-st cable

(decreases occur over 5 cables for two largest sizes, and over 3 cables for all other sizes), pick up and knit 10 (10, 11, 12, 11, 12, 13) sts down left front neck, place 6 (6, 7, 8, 9, 10, 11) sts from left front holder on needle and work in seed st as for right front—52 (52, 58, 64, 66, 68, 74) sts. Work 4 rows seed st. BO all sts in pattern on next row.

SLEEVES (make 2)
With larger needles, CO 36 (40, 44, 48, 48, 48, 52) sts and work in seed st for 14 (16, 18, 22, 24, 26, 28) rows. Change to smaller needles and work in seed st for 14 (16, 18, 22, 24, 26, 28) rows. Change to larger needles and continue in seed stitch, increasing 1 st at each side every 11 (15, 14, 14, 11, 8, 8) rows 4 (4, 5, 6, 6, 12, 3) times, then every 10 (0, 0, 0, 11, 0, 7) rows 1 (0, 0, 0, 3, 0, 11) time(s), ending with a RS row—46 (48, 54, 60, 66, 72, 80) sts, piece measures approximately 10¼ (11½, 13¼, 16, 18½, 18½, 19½)" from beginning. Set up cable pattern for sleeve on next row as follows: (WS) Work 2 (3, 6, 1, 4, 7, 3) sts seed st, *M1, p2, M1, 6 sts seed st; repeat from * a total of 5 (5, 5, 7, 7, 7, 9) times, M1, p2, M1, 2 (3, 6, 1, 4, 7, 3) sts seed st—58 (60, 66, 76, 82, 88, 100) sts.

Work seed and cable pattern as follows:
ROW 1: (RS) Work 2 (3, 6, 1, 4, 7, 3) sts seed st, *k4, 6 sts seed st; repeat from * a total of 5 (5, 5, 7, 7, 7, 9) times,

k4, 2 (3, 6, 1, 4, 7, 3) sts in seed st.
ROWS 2 AND 4: Work 2 (3, 6, 1, 4, 7, 3) sts seed st, *p4, 6 sts in seed st; repeat from * a total of 5 (5, 5, 7, 7, 7, 9) times, p4, 2 (3, 6, 1, 4, 7, 3) sts in seed st.
ROW 3: Work 2 (3, 6, 1, 4, 7, 3) sts seed st, *2/2LC, 6 sts in seed st; repeat from * a total of 5 (5, 5, 7, 7, 7, 9) times, 2/2LC, 2 (3, 6, 1, 4, 7, 3) sts seed st.

After working these 4 rows once, continue in pattern as established, increasing 1 st at each side every 7 (10, 11, 14, 9, 5, 5) rows 2 (2, 2, 2, 3, 5, 5) times, working increased sts in seed st—62 (64, 70, 80, 88, 98, 110) sts. Work even until piece measures 13¾ (16, 17½, 20½, 23½, 24¼, 25)" from beginning, ending with Row 4 of pattern. BO all sts on next row, working k2tog twice at the top of each 4-st cable.

FINISHING
Block pieces to finished measurements. Measure down 5½ (5¾, 6½, 7¼, 8, 9, 10)" from shoulder seam at each side of front and back and place markers. Sew upper edge of each sleeve between markers. Sew sleeve seams, reversing the lower 2½ (3, 3, 3½, 3½, 4, 4)" of seam so the RS of seam will show when cuffs are folded back. Sew side seams, leaving 1¾ (2, 2½, 3, 3¼, 3½, 4)" open at the bottom of each side seam for side slits. Weave in ends. Fold up cuffs 1¾ (2, 2¼, 2¾, 3, 3¼, 3½)", or to desired length.

finger puppets

PRISCILLA GIBSON-ROBERTS

Priscilla Gibson-Roberts created this masterful menagerie of finger puppets with her grandchildren in mind. She based her designs on the Old MacDonald and Mary Had a Little Lamb nursery rhymes, but there are certainly enough characters here for lots of different stories—both the classics you'll tell to children and the new ones you'll make up together.

Review notes on page 162 before beginning to knit.

General Directions

NECK AND SHOULDERS

Transfer held neck sts to needles. Knit 1 rnd (round) on 10 sts for the neck. On the following rnd, inc to 20 sts by knitting into the front and back of each st. Work two rnds of k1, p1 ribbing for shoulders.

BODY

When the shoulder ribbing has been completed, work body in the rnd on 20 stitches (for toddler to age 10), or inc 4 sts evenly to 24 sts in the first rnd (for age 10 to adult sizes). For very large adult fingers, change to the optional larger needles and work on 24 sts. Work even in St st until body measures desired length. Purl 1 rnd, knit 1 rnd. BO all sts in next rnd as if to purl. Weave in ends.

ARMS

Fold body in half vertically and identify the edge sts along the fold on each side. Beginning at the shoulder ribbing, using the same yarn as the body and a dpn, pick up and knit 4 sts by picking up in one half of each edge st for 4 rows. Turn body over, and with a second dpn pick up 4 sts in the same manner on the other side, from armpit to shoulder. Using a third dpn, work even in the rnd until arm measures approximately ¾" long. Stuff arm lightly, using the point of a knitting needle if necessary. Change to color for paw, hand, or hoof as desired, and knit 3 rnds. Break yarn, leaving a 6" tail. Draw tail through remaining sts and pull closed. Repeat for other arm. Weave in ends.

Finished Measurements
Puppets range from 2½" to 3" tall, and fit toddler to adult fingers.

Yarn
Røros Lamullgarn (100% lambswool; 274 yards / 50 grams): 1 skein each of L14 gray, L15 black, L12 white, L68 blue, L48 burgundy, L61 yellow, L56 medium pink, L46 magenta, L62 orange, L43 red, L82 navy blue, L12 silver-beige, L34 brown, L52 taupe, L94 green.

Needles
One set of five double-pointed needles (dpn) size US 0 (2 mm), 4" long needles are preferred.
One set of five dpn size US 3 (2.5 mm) if fitting very large adult fingers (optional).
Change needle size if necessary to obtain the correct gauge, although exact gauge is not essential for this project.

Notions
Polyester fiberfill or unspun wool for stuffing head and arms, small tapestry needle for weaving in ends and embroidering features, black buttonhole twist thread or craft thread for cat whiskers, small amounts of waste yarn for provisional cast-on, crochet hook size B/1 (2 mm).

Gauge
Approximately 10 sts and 14 rnds = 1" in Stockinette stitch (St st) in the rnd.

notes

These seamless finger puppets require a number of advanced knitting skills. For the faint-of-heart, they have been arranged in order of difficulty, beginning with the burro, and working up to the red hen. Follow the directions for your chosen character, referring to the General Directions as required. All of the puppets are worked top down, from head to base.

Ssk (slip, slip, knit): Slip the next 2 sts to right-hand needle one at a time as if to knit, return these 2 sts to the left-hand needle one at a time in their new orientation, and knit them together through the back of their loops.

Ssp (slip, slip, purl): Slip the next 2 sts to right-hand needle one at a time as if to knit, pass these 2 sts back to the left-hand needle one at a time in their new orientation, and purl them together through the back of their loops.

Sssp (slip, slip, slip, purl): Slip the next 3 sts to right-hand needle one at a time as if to knit, pass these 3 sts back to the left-hand needle one at a time in their new orientation, and purl them together through the back of their loops.

M1 (make 1, right-slanting): Insert tip of left-hand needle under the strand between the two needles, from back to front, and lift this strand onto the left-hand needle. Knit the lifted strand through the front of its loop to increase 1 st.

Yo (yarnover, conventional method): Bring yarn to the front and over the right-hand needle. Work the newly-created loop as a st on the next row.

K1tbl: Knit one through the back of its loop.

Yarnover Back to Front: With the purl side of work facing, bring yarn to the back under the right-hand needle, then bring yarn to front over the right-hand needle. Work the newly-created loop as instructed in the pattern.

Provisional Cast-On: Using a thin, smooth scrap yarn, CO the required number of sts and work in Stockinette st (St st) for 3–4 rows. Change to main yarn and continue as directed.

Emily Ocker's Circular Cast-On: Form a circle of thread around one or two fingers. Using a crochet hook and the end of the yarn attached to the yarn supply (not the short tail), *pull up a loop through the center of the circle and leave it on the hook, yarn over hook; repeat from * until you have the required number of sts on the hook. Transfer these sts to dpns, and work them through the back of their loops on the first rnd (round). After several rnds have been completed, pull the tail at the beginning of the cast-on and close the center of the circle snugly.

I-Cord: Using dpns, knit all sts, *slide the work to the opposite end of the needle, bring yarn around behind sts, and knit them again from the same direction (working yarn is pulled up from bottom stitch to top stitch when you start a new row); repeat from * for as many rows as indicated.

Backward Loop Cast-On: Make a loop in the working yarn and place on the right-hand needle, oriented so that it doesn't unwind, to increase 1 st.

Colors used for characters shown:

BURRO – gray, black, white, small amount of blue for eyes

BULL – burgundy, yellow, small amount of black and white for face

PIG – medium pink, magenta, small amount of black, white, and blue for face

LARGE CAT – orange, gray, black, white, small amount of yellow for eyes

SMALL CAT – yellow, black, orange, small amount of black and green for face

LAMB – white, silver-beige, black, small amount of red and blue for face

OLD MACDONALD – black, red, navy blue, yellow, small amount of white for eyes

MARY – taupe, brown, orange, magenta, small amount of black and white for eyes

DUCK – green, black, gray, small amount of yellow and orange for bill

RED HEN – red, black, small amount of yellow and white for beak and eyes

Burro

HEAD

Beginning at tip of nose using white, CO 10 sts onto one dpn, using provisional cast-on with waste yarn (see Notes). Work short row shaping to form the nose as follows, working yo (yarnovers; see Notes) in the conventional manner unless otherwise specified:

ROW 1: (RS) K9, turn (1 st remains unworked at end of needle).

ROW 2: Yo back to front (see Notes), p8, turn (1 st remains unworked at other end of needle).

ROW 3: Yo, k7, turn.

ROW 4: Yo back to front, p6, turn.

ROW 5: Yo, k5, turn.

ROW 6: Yo back to front, p4, turn.

ROW 7: Yo, k4, correct the stitch mount of the next yo, k2tog (the yo and st after it), turn.

ROW 8: Yo back to front, p5, ssp (see Notes), turn.

ROW 9: Yo, k6, correct the stitch mount of the next 2 yo's, k3tog (the yo's and st after them), turn.

ROW 10: Yo back to front, p7, sssp (see Notes), turn.

ROW 11: Yo, k8, correct the stitch mount of the next 2 yo's, k3tog (the yo's and the st after them), turn.

ROW 12: Sl (slip) the first st as if to purl with yarn in front, p8, sssp—10 sts.

Carefully remove waste yarn from provisional cast-on, place 10 live sts from base of cast on on a second dpn, and knit across these sts—20 sts. With sts divided as evenly as possible on 2 needles, and using a third needle for working, knit 1 rnd on all sts using white. Change to gray and knit 1 rnd. Increase Rnd: On first needle, k10 (top of nose); on the second needle (sides of face and underside of jaw) k1, M1 (see Notes), knit to last st of rnd, M1, k1—2 sts increased. Repeat the increase rnd 4 more times, dividing the sts for the sides of the face onto 2 needles when there are too many sts to work them on a single needle—30 sts, 10 on a single needle for the top of the nose, and 10 sts each on two needles for sides of face.

TURN THE HEAD

Work back and forth in rows, as you would to turn a square sock heel. If desired, you can transfer the sts to be worked together to the same needle before working the decreases.

ROW 1: K9, ssk (last st of first needle and first st of next needle, see Notes), turn.

ROW 2: Sl 1 as if to purl with yarn in front, p8, p2tog (last st of working needle and first st of next needle), turn.

ROW 3: Sl 1 as if to purl with yarn in back, k8, ssk (last st of working needle and first st of next needle).

Repeat Rows 2 and 3 until only 10 sts remain on first needle, and all sts on the other needles have been decreased away. Place remaining sts on a holder or waste yarn temporarily while you complete the head.

HEAD FINISHING

Stuff head lightly, using eraser end of a pencil to maneuver fiber into contours of head, and embroider facial features, entering and exiting through neck opening as you work embroidery. Embroider mouth, nostrils, and eyes using white, black, and blue as shown in photograph. Embroidery yarn tails should be zigzagged through stuffing several times to secure stuffing and yarn ends.

EARS

With the back of the head facing you and using gray, pick up and knit up 5 sts from the corner of the head turning toward the center of the top of the head. Work 7 rows St st, beginning and ending with a purl row. Beginning with next row, shape ear as follows: Ssk, k1, k2tog, turn, p3, turn, sl 2 sts as if to k2tog, k1, pass 2 slipped sts over—1 st remains. Break yarn and draw through last st. Weave the end in along edge of ear. Repeat for other ear. Coax ears upright as shown.

MANE

Cut twelve 4" strands of black yarn. Using 2 strands held together, fold strands in half, and use a crochet hook to draw loop through top of head, centered between the ears. Pull ends through the loop and tighten, making a fringe knot. Make another 2-strand fringe knot in front of the first, and four more fringe knots down the back of the neck. Trim ends to ½" long, tease open the plies to create a bushy mane, and style the front knot to hang toward the face like a forelock.

BODY AND ARMS

Transfer 10 held sts to needles, and using gray, complete neck, and shoulders as given in General Directions. Work body according to General Directions on 20 or 24 sts, depending on your size, until body measures 2" from beginning of neck. Work arms in gray and hooves in black according to General Directions.

Bull

HEAD

Using yellow, work short-rowed nose as for burro, then work 1 rnd with yellow on all sts. Change to burgundy and work face as for burro. Turn the head as for burro. Stuff head with fiber. Embroider mouth, nostrils, and eyes using black and white as shown in photograph.

EARS

Using burgundy and the back of the head facing you, pick up and knit up 7 sts from the corner of the head turning down along the side of the turned flap. Work 5 rows St st, beginning and ending with a purl row. Next row: Ssk, k3, k2tog—5 sts. Purl 1 row. Next row: Ssk, k1, k2tog—3 sts. Break yarn and draw through all sts. Weave the end in along edge of ear. Repeat for other ear. Coax ears into sticking out horizontally as shown.

HORNS

Using yellow, pick up and knit 3 sts on top of head near base of ear. Work I-cord (see Notes) for 3 rows. Break yarn and draw through all sts. Weave end down into the center of the horn, pulling slightly to make horn curve. Repeat for other horn.

NECK, SHOULDERS, BODY, AND ARMS

Using burgundy, complete neck and shoulders as given in General Directions. Work body according to General Directions on 20 or 24 sts, depending on your size, until body measures 2" from beginning of neck. Work arms in burgundy and hooves in yellow according to General Directions.

Pig

HEAD

Using magenta, CO 3 sts using Emily Ocker's circular cast-on (see Notes). On first rnd, *k1tbl (see Notes), CO 1 using backward loop cast-on (see Notes); repeat from * 2 times—6 sts. Work each backward loop CO st through the back of loop on the following rnd to avoid leaving a hole. On second round, *k1, CO 1 using backward loop cast-on; repeat from * 5 times—12 sts. Knit 1 rnd, purl 1 rnd.

Pull tail of cast-on gently to close starting circle. Change to medium pink. Divide sts evenly on 2 needles, and using a third needle for working, knit 1 rnd on all sts. Increase Rnd: On first needle, k6 (top of nose); on the second needle (sides of face and underside of jaw) k1, M1 (see Notes), knit to last st of rnd, M1, k1—2 sts increased. Next rnd: P6 (top of nose), knit to end. Repeat the last 2 rnds 2 times, dividing the sts for the sides of the face onto 2 needles when there are too many sts to work them on a single needle—18 sts, 6 on a single needle for the top of the nose, and 6 sts each on two needles for sides of face. Next rnd: Knit into the front and back of the first 5 sts, k1 (11 sts on needle for top of nose), k12—23 sts. Increase Rnd: K1, M1, knit to last st on first needle, M1, k1, knit to end—2 sts increased, 25 sts. Repeat the increase rnd 2 more times—29 sts. Work one rnd as follows: K1, M1, k8, M1, k7, M1, k1, knit to end—30 sts. Turn the head as for burro. Stuff head with fiber. Embroider mouth, nostrils, and eyes using black, white, and blue as shown in photograph.

EARS

Using medium pink and the back of the head facing you, pick up and knit 5 sts from the corner of the head turning toward the center of the top of the head. Purl 1 row, knit 1 row, purl 1 row. Next row: Ssk (see Notes), k1, k2tog—3 sts. Purl 1 row. Next row: Sl (slip) 2 as if to k2tog, k1, pass 2 slipped sts over—1 st. Break yarn and fasten off. Weave the end in along edge of ear. Repeat for other ear. Coax ears into sticking upright as shown.

NECK, SHOULDERS, BODY, AND ARMS

Using medium pink, complete neck and shoulders as given in General Directions. Work body according to General Directions on 20 or 24 sts, depending on your size, until body measures 2" from beginning of neck. Work arms in medium pink according to General Directions. Work hooves in black; knit the first rnd, then purl all successive rnds.

Large Cat

HEAD

Using orange, CO 5 sts using Emily Ocker's circular cast-on (see Notes). On first rnd, *k1tbl (see Notes), CO 1 using backward loop cast-on (see Notes); repeat from * 4 times—10 sts. Work each backward loop CO st through the back of loop on the following rnd to avoid leaving a hole. Divide sts evenly on 2 needles, and using a third needle for working, knit 1 rnd on all sts. Pull tail of cast-on gently to close starting circle. Shape face as follows, dividing the sts for the top of the nose onto 2 needles when there are too many sts to work them

on a single needle, and work yo (see Notes) increases through the back of their loops on the following rnd:

RND 1: On first needle (top of nose) k2, yo, k1, yo, k2; on second needle, knit to end—12 sts.

RND 2: K3, yo, k1, yo, k3 (top of nose); knit to end (underside of jaw)—14 sts.

RND 3: K4, yo, k1, yo, k4 (top of nose); k1, M1 (see Notes), knit to last st, M1, k1—18 sts.

RND 4: On top of nose, knit to center st, yo, k1, yo, knit to end of needle; knit to end—2 sts increased.

RNDS 5 – 9: Repeat Rnd 4. There will be 30 sts after completing Rnd 9—23 sts for top of nose, and 7 sts for underside of jaw.

Work short rows as follows:

ROW 1: Yo, k24, turn.

ROW 2: Yo back to front (see Notes), p25, turn.

ROW 3: Sl (slip) the first st as if to purl with yarn in back, knit to yo, correct the stitch mount of the yo, k2tog (the yo and the st after it), turn.

ROW 4: Sl the first st as if to purl with yarn in front, purl to yo, ssp (the yo and the st after it, see Notes), turn—30 sts.

Break yarn. Rearrange sts on four needles as follows: 11 sts for top of head (the single st between the yo increases should at the center of the needle), 7 sts for side of face, 5 sts for underside of jaw, 7 sts for other side of face. Rejoin yarn at beginning of 11-st needle for top of head.

TURN THE HEAD

Work back and forth in rows, as you would to turn a square sock heel. If desired, you can transfer the sts to be worked together to the same needle before working the decreases.

ROW 1: K10, ssk (last st of first needle and first st of next needle, see Notes), turn.

ROW 2: Sl 1 as if to purl with yarn in front, p9, p2tog (last st of working needle and first st of next needle), turn.

ROW 3: Sl 1 as if to purl with yarn in back, k9, ssk (last st of working needle and first st of next needle).

Repeat Rows 2 and 3 until 11 sts remain on needle for top of head, 5 sts remain on needle for underside of jaw, and all sts on the other needles have been decreased away—16 sts. Work next rnd on all sts as follows: (k1, k2tog twice) 2 times, k2, sl 2 sts as to k2tog, k1, pass 2 slipped sts over, k1—10 sts. Place sts on a holder or waste yarn temporarily while you complete the head.

Stuff head with fiber. Embroider mouth, nostrils, and eyes using black, white, and yellow as shown in photograph. Using gray, embroider tiger stripe on right cheek as shown. Using buttonhole twist thread, make whiskers. Work ears as for pig, using orange for the right ear, and gray for the left ear.

Using orange, complete neck and shoulders as given in General Directions. Work body according to General Directions on 20 or 24 sts, depending on your size, until body measures 2" from beginning of neck. Work left arm in gray, and right arm in stripes of orange and white as shown, according to General Directions. Work paws in black. Embroider tiger stripes of gray and white on body and right arm as shown.

TAIL

Using white, pick up and knit 3 sts above the garter st edge at bottom of body. Work I-cord (see Notes) tail on 3 sts as follows: 20 rows white, 2 rows gray, 10 rows orange. Weave end 1" down into the center of tail, then bring it to the outside of tail, and use the end to tack the tail to the body as shown.

Small Cat

HEAD

Using yellow, CO 5 sts using Emily Ocker's circular cast-on (see Notes). On first rnd, *k1tbl (see Notes), CO 1 using backward loop cast-on (see Notes); repeat from * 4 times—10 sts. Work each backward loop CO st through the back loop on the following rnd to avoid leaving a hole. Divide sts evenly on 2 needles, and using a third needle for working, knit 1 rnd on all sts. Pull tail of cast-on gently to close starting circle. Shape face as follows, dividing the sts for the top of the nose onto 2 needles when there are too many sts to work them on a single needle, and work yo (see Notes) increases through the back of

their loops on the following row:

RND 1: On first needle (top of nose) k2, yo, k1, yo, k2; on second needle, knit to end—12 sts.

RND 2: K3, yo, k1, yo, k3 (top of nose); knit to end (underside of jaw)—14 sts.

RND 3: K4, yo, k1, yo, k4 (top of nose); k1, M1 (see Notes), knit to last st, M1, k1—18 sts.

RND 4: On top of nose, knit to center st, yo, k1, yo, knit to end of needle; knit to end—2 sts increased.

RNDS 5 – 7: Repeat Rnd 4. There will be 26 sts after completing Rnd 7—19 sts for top of nose, and 7 sts for underside of jaw.

Work short rows as follows:
ROW 1: Yo, k20, turn.
ROW 2: Yo back to front (see Notes), p21, turn.
ROW 3: Sl (slip) the first st as if to purl with yarn in back, knit to yo, correct the stitch mount of the yo, k2tog (the yo and the st after it), turn.
ROW 4: Sl the first st as if to purl with yarn in front, purl to yo, ssp (the yo and the st after it, see Notes), turn—26 sts.

Break yarn. Rearrange sts on four needles as follows: 9 sts for top of head (the single st between the yo

increases should at the center of the needle), 6 sts for side of face, 5 sts for underside of jaw, 6 sts for other side of face. Rejoin yarn at beginning of 9-st needle for top of head.

TURN THE HEAD

Work back and forth in rows, as you would to turn a square sock heel. If desired, you can transfer the sts to be worked together to the same needle before working the decreases.

ROW 1: K8, ssk (last st of first needle and first st of next needle, see Notes), turn.

ROW 2: Sl 1 as if to purl with yarn in front, p7, p2tog (last st of working needle and first st of next needle), turn.

ROW 3: Sl 1 as if to purl with yarn in back, k7, ssk (last st of working needle and first st of next needle).

Repeat Rows 2 and 3 until 9 sts remain on needle for top of head, 5 sts remain on needle for underside of jaw, and all sts on the other needles have been decreased away—14 sts. Work next rnd on all sts as follows: k2, k2tog, k1, k2tog, k3, sl 2 sts as to k2tog, k1, pass 2 slipped sts over, k1—10 sts. Place sts on a holder or waste yarn temporarily while you complete the head.

Stuff head with fiber. Embroider mouth, nostrils, and eyes using black and green as shown in photograph. Using orange, embroider tiger stripes on top and back of head as shown. With buttonhole twist thread, make whiskers. With yellow, work ears as for pig.

NECK, SHOULDERS, BODY, AND ARMS

With yellow, complete neck and shoulders as given in General Directions. Work body according to General Directions on 20 or 24 sts, depending on your size, until body measures 1¾" from beginning of neck. Work arms in yellow with black paws, according to General Directions. Embroider tiger stripes of orange on body as shown. With yellow throughout, work 28 rows of I-cord (see Notes) for tail as for large cat. Attach tail to body as for large cat.

Lamb

HEAD

Using black, CO 5 sts using Emily Ocker's circular cast-on (see Notes). Knit 1 rnd through back loops. Next rnd: *K1, CO 1 using backward loop cast-on (see Notes); repeat from * 4 times—10 sts. Work each backward loop CO st through the back of loop on the following rnd to avoid leaving a hole. Knit 1 rnd. Next rnd: *K2, CO 1 using backward loop cast-on; repeat from * 4 times—15 sts. Knit 1 rnd.

Work short rows as follows, working yo (yarnovers, see Notes) in the conventional manner unless otherwise specified:

ROW 1: K10, turn.

ROW 2: Yo back to front (see Notes) p5, turn.

ROW 3: Yo, k5, correct the stitch mount of the yo, k2tog (yo and st after it), k1, turn.

ROW 4: Yo back to front, p7, ssp (yo and st after it, see Notes), p1, turn.

ROW 5: Yo, k9, correct the stitch mount of the yo, k2tog (yo and st after it), k1, turn.

ROW 6: Yo back to front, p11, ssp, p1, turn.

ROW 7: Yo, k13, k2tog (yo and st after it), k1—17 sts.

Change to silver-beige and work 1 rnd on all sts, working yarnovers

through the back of loops. Break yarn. Rearrange sts on four needles as follows: 2 sts (the first and last sts of the rnd) on one needle for underside of jaw, 5 sts each on two needles for sides of face, and 5 sts on a single needle for top of head. Rejoin yarn at beginning of 5-st needle for top of head.

TURN THE HEAD

Work back and forth in rows, as you would to turn a square sock heel. If desired, you can transfer the sts to be worked together to the same needle before working the decreases.

ROW 1: K4, ssk (last st of first needle and first st of next needle, see Notes), turn.

ROW 2: Sl (slip) 1 as if to purl with yarn in front, p3, p2tog (last st of working needle and first st of next needle), turn.

ROW 3: Sl 1 as if to purl with yarn in back, k3, ssk (last st of working needle and first st of next needle)

Repeat Rows 2 and 3 until 5 sts remain on needle for top of head, 2 sts remain on needle for underside of jaw, and all sts on the other needles have

been decreased away—7 sts. Knit 1 rnd, increasing 3 sts—10 sts. Place sts on a holder or waste yarn temporarily while you complete the head.

Stuff head with fiber. Embroider mouth, nostrils, and eyes using red, white, and blue as shown in photograph.

EARS

Using black and the back of the head facing you, pick up and knit up 5 sts from the corner of the head turning down along the side of the turned flap. Work 5 rows St st, beginning and ending with a purl row. Next row: Ssk, k1, k2tog—3 sts. Break yarn and draw through all sts. Weave the end in along edge of ear. Repeat for other ear. Coax ears into sticking out horizontally as shown.

NECK, SHOULDERS, BODY, AND ARMS

Using silver-beige, complete neck and shoulders as given in General Directions. Change to white and work body according to General Directions on 20 or 24 sts, depending on your size, until body measures 1¾" from beginning of neck. Work arms in white and hooves in black according to General Directions.

Old MacDonald

HAT AND HEAD

Using yellow, CO 8 sts using Emily Ocker's circular cast-on (see Notes). Knit 1 rnd through back of loops. Next rnd: *K1, CO 1 using backward loop cast-on (see Notes); repeat from * 7 times—16 sts. Work each backward loop CO st through the back of loop on the following rnd to avoid leaving a hole. Knit 1 rnd. Next rnd: *K1, CO 1

using backward loop cast-on, k3; repeat from * 3 times—20 sts. Knit 1 rnd. Next rnd: *K1, CO 1 using backward loop cast-on, k4; repeat from * 3 times—24 sts. Knit 5 rnds. Change to red and knit 1 rnd for hatband. Change to yellow, knit 1 rnd, purl 1 rnd. Re-arrange on three needles as follows: 6 sts on first needle for side and back of head, 12 sts for front of face, 6 sts for other side and back of head.

Change to black and work short rows as follows, working yo (yarnovers; see Notes) in the conventional manner unless otherwise specified:

ROW 1: K14, turn.

ROW 2: Yo back to front (see Notes) p4, turn.

ROW 3: Yo, k4, correct the stitch mount of the yo, k2tog (yo and st after it), k3, turn.

ROW 4: Yo back to front, p8, ssp (yo and st after it, see Notes), p3, turn.

ROW 5: Yo, k12, correct the stitch mount of the yo, k2tog (yo and st after it), k3, turn.

ROW 6: Yo back to front, p16, ssp, p3, turn.

ROW 7: Yo, k20, k2tog (yo and st after it), k1.

Work 1 rnd on all sts as follows: K1, k2tog (last remaining yo and st before it), knit to end—24 sts, beginning of rnd is at center back of head.

Shape chin and neck as follows:

RND 1: K10, ssk (see Notes), k2tog, k10—22 sts.

RND 2: K2, [k2tog, k2] 5 times—17 sts.

RND 3: K6, ssk, k1, k2tog, k6—15 sts.

RND 4: [K1, k2tog] 5 times—10 sts.

RND 5: Knit all sts.

Place all sts on a holder or waste yarn temporarily while you complete the head. Stuff head with fiber. Embroider eyes and mouth using red, blue, and white as shown in photograph.

HAT BRIM

With yellow and beginning at center back of head, pick up and knit 24 sts in the purl heads of the sts in the yellow purl rnd. Purl 1 rnd. Next rnd: Knit, increasing 6 sts evenly spaced—30 sts. Purl 1 rnd. BO as if to knit on next rnd. Tack brim to back of head when weaving in the ends.

NECK, SHOULDERS, BODY, AND ARMS

Change to red and complete neck and shoulders as given in General Directions. Work body according to General Directions on 20 or 24 sts, depending on your size, until red section measures 1". Change to navy blue and work even until body measures 2" from neck, then finish according to General Directions. Work arms in red for 6 rnds, purl 1 rnd red, then change to black and knit 6 rnds for hands, according to General Directions.

Mary

HAIR AND HEAD

Using taupe, CO 8 sts using Emily Ocker's circular cast-on (see Notes). Knit 1 rnd through back of loops. Next rnd: *K1, CO 1 using backward loop cast-on (see Notes); repeat from * 7 more times—16 sts. Work each backward loop CO st through the back loop on the following rnd to avoid leaving a hole. Knit 1 rnd. Next rnd: *K1, CO 1 using backward loop cast-on, k3; repeat from * 3 more times—20 sts. Knit 1 rnd. Next rnd: *K1, CO 1 using backward loop cast-on, k4; repeat from * 3 more times—24 sts. Knit 5 rnds. Next rnd: Join brown and work 1 rnd *k1 brown, k1 taupe; repeat from * to end. Rearrange sts on three needles as follows: 6 sts on first needle for side and back of head, 12 sts for front of face, 6 sts for other side and back of head.

Continue with brown only, and work short rows as follows, working yo (yarnovers, see Notes) in the conventional manner unless otherwise specified:

ROW 1: K14, turn.

ROW 2: Yo back to front (see Notes) p4, turn.

ROW 3: Yo, k4, correct the stitch mount of the yo, k2tog (yo and st after it), k3, turn.

ROW 4: Yo back to front, p8, ssp (yo and st after it, see Notes), p3, turn.

ROW 5: Yo, k12, correct the stitch mount of the yo, k2tog (yo and st after it), k3, turn.

ROW 6: Yo back to front, p16, ssp, p3, turn.

ROW 7: Yo, k20, k2tog (yo and st after it), k1.

Work 1 rnd on all sts as follows: K1, k2tog (last remaining yo and st before it), knit to end—24 sts, beginning of rnd is at center back of head.

Shape chin and neck as follows:

RND 1: K10, ssk (see Notes), k2tog, k10—22 sts.

RND 2: K2, [k2tog, k2] 5 times—17 sts.

RND 3: K6, ssk, k1, k2tog, k6—15 sts.

RND 4: [K1, k2tog] 5 times—10 sts.

RND 5: Knit all sts.

Place all sts on a holder or yarn temporarily while you complete the head. Stuff head with fiber. Embroider eyes, mouth, and earrings using black, white, magenta, and orange as shown in photograph. Embroider bun on top of head with taupe.

Knit 2 rnds brown. On the next rnd, inc to 20 sts by knitting into the front and back of each st. Work two rnds of k1, p1 ribbing for shoulders. Knit 1 rnd.

RUFFLE

Change to magenta and work 1 rnd knitting into the front and back of each st—40 sts. Next rnd: *K1, purl in front and back of next st; repeat from * to end—60 sts. Work 8 rnds even (knit the knits and purl the purls). Change to orange and work even for 2 rnds. BO all sts as they appear.

DRESS AND ARMS

Turn ruffle up over head, and using magenta, pick up and knit 1 st in each st at base of brown k1, p1 rnd—20 sts. Work 10 rnds magenta on 20 or 24 sts according to General Directions. On the next rnd, join orange and work 1 rnd *k1 magenta, k1 orange; repeat from * to end. On the following rnd: *k1 orange, k1 magenta; repeat from * to end. Repeat the last 2 rnds until body measures 2" from neck. Using orange only, complete body according to General Directions. Using brown, work arms and hands according to General Directions.

Duck

BILL AND HEAD

Using waste yarn, CO 5 sts. Sl (slip) all sts as if to purl, with yarn in front; set up for double knitting as follows:

ROW 1: K1, sl 1, k1, sl 1, k1.

ROW 2: Sl 1, k1, sl 1, k1, sl 1.

Work Rows 1 and 2 twice with waste yarn. Change to yellow and work Rows 1 and 2 seven times, ending with Row 2—14 rows total. Carefully remove waste yarn, draw tail of yellow yarn through the loops, pull gently to close.

Arrange sts on 2 needles with Sts 1, 3, and 5 of Row 1 on one needle, and the other 2 sts on another—5 sts. Change to orange and knit 1 rnd. Change to green. Next rnd: *K1, M1

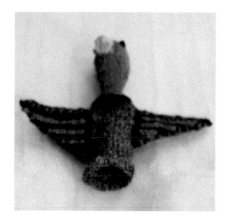

(see Notes); repeat from * around—10 sts. Knit 2 rnds.

Shape face as follows, dividing the sts for the top of the bill onto 2 needles when there are too many sts to work them on a single needle:

RND 1: On first needle (bottom of bill) k2, yo (see Notes), k3; on second needle (top of bill), *k1, M1; repeat from * to end—16 sts.

RNDS 2 - 4: Knit

RND 5: On first needle, k6; on top of bill, [k1, M1] 4 times, k2, [M1, k1] 4 times—24 sts.

RNDS 6 – 8: Knit.

Break yarn. Rearrange sts on four needles as follows: 4 sts for center bottom of bill, 6 sts for side of face, 8 sts for center top of bill, 6 sts for other side of face. Rejoin yarn at beginning of 8-st needle for top of bill.

TURN THE HEAD

Work back and forth in rows, as you would to turn a square sock heel. If desired, you can transfer the sts to be worked together to the same needle before working the decreases.

ROW 1: K7, ssk (last st of first needle and first st of next needle, see Notes), turn.

ROW 2: Sl 1 as if to purl with yarn in front, p6, p2tog (last st of working needle and first st of next needle), turn.

ROW 3: Sl 1 as if to purl with yarn in back, k6, ssk (last st of working needle and first st of next needle). Repeat Rows 2 and 3 until 8 sts remain on needle for top of head, 4 sts remain on needle for bottom of bill, and all sts on the other needles have been decreased away—12 sts. Work next rnd on all sts as follows: k8 for top of head; k2tog, ssk on bottom of bill—10 sts. Knit 4 rnds. Place sts on a holder or waste yarn temporarily while you complete the head.

Stuff head with fiber. Embroider eyes with black as shown in photograph.

NECK, SHOULDERS, AND BODY

Change to black and knit 1 rnd. On the next rnd, increase to 20 sts by knitting into the front and back of each st. Work two rnds of k1, p1 ribbing for shoulders. Change to gray and work body on 20 or 24 sts, according to General Directions, until gray section measures 1½". Finish body according to General Directions.

WINGS

Identify edge sts along the fold at each side as for arms. With black, pick up and knit 9 sts from shoulder to "wingpit" by picking up in one half of each edge st every other row. Turn body over and pick up 9 sts from wingpit to shoulder on the other side—18 sts. Arrange sts on one needle, alternating a st from the side facing you with a st from the other side, with a purl st from the side farthest away from you as the first st to be worked. Beginning at the shoulder side

of the wing, and slipping all sts as if to purl, work in two-color double-knitting as follows:

ROW 1: With black, p1, [k1, p1, sl 1 yb (with yarn in back), sl 1 yf (with yarn in front)] 4 times, k1. Turn.

ROW 2: With green, repeat Row 1. Slide work to opposite end of needle, ready to use black for the next row.

ROW 3: With black, p2tog, sl 1 yf, [k1, p1, sl 1 yb, sl 1 yf] 3 times, k1, p1, k1—17 sts. Turn.

ROW 4: With green, p1, [sl 1 yb, sl 1 yf, k1, p1] 3 times, sl 1 yb, sl 1 yf, k2tog—16 sts. Slide.

ROW 5: With black, p1, [k1, p1, sl 1 yb, sl 1 yf] 3 times, k1, k2tog—15 sts. Turn.

ROW 6: With green, p2tog, [k1, p1, sl 1 yb, sl 1 yf] 3 times, k1—14 sts. Slide.

ROW 7: With black, p2tog, sl 1 yf, [k1, p1, sl 1 yb, sl 1 yf] 2 times, k1, p1, k1—13 sts. Turn.

ROW 8: With green, p1, [sl 1 yb, sl 1 yf, k1, p1] 2 times, sl 1 yb, sl 1 yf, k2tog—12 sts. Slide.

ROW 9: With black, p1, [k1, p1, sl 1 yb, sl 1 yf] 2 times, k1, k2tog—11 sts. Turn.

ROW 10: With green, p2tog, [k1, p1, sl 1 yb, sl 1 yf] 2 times, k1—10 sts. Slide.

ROW 11: With black, p2tog, sl 1 yf, k1, p1, sl 1 yb, sl 1 yf, k1, p1, k1—9 sts. Turn.

ROW 12: With green, p1, sl 1 yb, sl 1 yf, k1, p1, sl 1 yb, sl 1 yf, k2tog—8 sts. Slide.

ROW 13: With black, p1, k1, p1, sl 1 yb, sl 1 yf, k1, k2tog—7 sts. Turn.

ROW 14: With green, p2tog, k1, p1, sl 1 yb, sl 1 yf, k1—6 sts. Slide.

ROW 15: With black, p2tog, sl 1 yb, sl 1 yf, k1, p1, k1—5 sts. Turn.

ROW 16: With green, p1, sl 1 yb, sl 1 yf, k2tog—4 sts. Slide. Break off green.

ROW 17: With black, sl 2 sts as if to k2tog (knit 2 together), k2tog, pass 2 slipped sts over—1 st. Fasten off.

Repeat for other wing, reversing colors, if desired, to make the second wing a mirror image of the first. Weave in ends.

Red Hen

HEAD

Using yellow, CO 5 sts using Emily Ocker's circular cast-on (see Notes). Knit 1 rnd through back of loops. Next rnd: *K1, CO 1 using backward loop cast-on (see Notes); repeat from * 4 more times—10 sts. Work each backward loop CO st through the back of loop on the following rnd to avoid leaving a hole. Change to red. Shape face as follows, dividing the sts for the top of the beak onto 2 needles when there are too many sts to work them on a single needle:

RND 1: On first needle (bottom of beak) k2, yo (see Notes), k3; on second needle (top of beak), *k1, M1 (see Notes); repeat from * to end—16 sts.

RNDS 2–4: Knit

RND 5: On first needle, k6; on top of beak, [k1, M1] 4 times, k2, [M1, k1] 4 times—24 sts.

RNDS 6–8: Knit.

Break yarn. Rearrange sts on four needles as follows: 4 sts for center bottom of beak, 6 sts for side of face, 8 sts for center top of beak, 6 sts for other side of face. Rejoin yarn at beginning of 8-st needle for top of beak.

TURN THE HEAD

Work back and forth in rows, as you would to turn a square sock heel. If

desired, you can transfer the sts to be worked together to the same needle before working the decreases.

ROW 1: K7, ssk (last st of first needle and first st of next needle, see Notes), turn.

ROW 2: Sl (slip) 1 as if to purl yf (with yarn in front), p6, p2tog (last st of working needle and first st of next needle), turn.

ROW 3: Sl 1 as if to purl yb (with yarn in back), k6, ssk (last st of working needle and first st of next needle). Repeat Rows 2 and 3 until 8 sts remain on needle for top of head, 4 sts remain on needle for bottom of beak, and all sts on the other needles have been decreased away—12 sts. Work next rnd on all sts as follows: k8 for top of head; k2tog, ssk on bottom of beak—10 sts. Knit 1 rnd. Place sts on a holder or waste yarn temporarily while you complete the head.

Stuff head with fiber. Embroider nostrils, eyes, and crest with black and white as shown in photograph.

NECK, SHOULDERS, AND BODY
Change to red and knit 1 rnd, increasing to 20 sts by knitting into the front and back of each st. Work two rnds of k1, p1 ribbing for shoulders. Work body on 20 or 24 sts, according to General Directions, until body measures 1¾" from neck. Finish body according to General Directions.

WINGS
Identify edge sts along the fold at each side as for arms. With black, pick up and knit 9 sts from shoulder to "wingpit" by picking up in one half of each edge st every other row. Turn body over and pick up 9 sts from wingpit to shoulder on the other side—18 sts. Arrange sts on one needle, alternating a st from the side facing you with a st from the other side, with a knit st from the side closest to you as the first st to be worked. Beginning at the shoulder, and slipping all sts as if to purl, work in two-color double-knitting as follows:

ROW 1: With red, k1, *[k1, sl 1 yf] 2 times, [sl 1 yb, p1] 2 times; repeat from * 1 more time, k1. Slide work to opposite end of needle, ready to use black for the next row.

ROW 2: With black, k1, *[sl 1 yb, p1] 2 times, [k1, sl 1 yf] 2 times; repeat from * 1 more time, k1. Turn.

ROW 3: With black, k1, *[sl 1 yb, p1] 2 times, [k1, sl 1 yf] 2 times; repeat from * 1 more time, k1. Slide.

ROW 4: With red, k1, *[k1, sl 1 yf] 2 times, [sl 1 yb, p1] 2 times; repeat from * 1 more time, k1. Turn.

ROW 5: With red, repeat Row 1. Slide.

ROW 6: With black, repeat Row 2.

ROW 7: BO 4 sts, working each BO st in its matching color (1 black st on right-hand needle). With black, [sl 1 yb, p1] 2 times, [k1, sl 1 yf] 2 times, [sl 1 yb, p1] 2 times, k1—14 sts. Slide.

ROW 8: With red, k1, [k1, sl 1 yf] 2 times, [sl 1 yb, p1] 2 times, [k1, sl 1 yf] 2 times, k1. Turn.

ROW 9: With red, k1, [sl 1 yb, p1] 2 times, [k1, sl 1 yf] 2 times, [sl 1 yb, p1] 2 times, k1. Slide.

ROW 10: With black, k1, [k1, sl 1 yf] 2 times, [sl 1 yb, p1] 2 times, [k1, sl 1 yf] 2 times, k1. Turn.

ROW 11: With black, k1, [sl 1 yb, p1] 2 times, [k1, sl 1 yf] 2 times, [sl 1 yb, p1] 2 times, k1. Slide.

ROW 12: With red, BO 4 sts, [sl 1 yb, p1] 2 times, [k1, sl 1 yf] 2 times, k1—10 sts. Turn.

ROW 13: With red, k1, [k1, sl 1 yf] 2 times, [sl 1 yb, p1] 2 times, k1. Slide.

ROW 14: With black, k1, [sl 1 yb, p1] 2 times, [k1, sl 1 yf] 2 times, k1. Turn.

ROW 15: With black, repeat Row 14. Slide.

ROW 16: With red, repeat Row 13. Turn.

ROW 17: With red, repeat Row 13. Slide.

ROW 18: With black, repeat Row 14. Turn.

ROW 19: BO 4 sts, working each BO st in its matching color (1 black st on right-hand needle). With black, [sl 1 yb, p1] 2 times, k1—6 sts. Slide.

ROW 20: With red, k1, [k1, sl 1 yf] 2 times, k1. Turn.

ROW 21: With red, k1, [sl 1 yb, p1] 2 times, k1. Slide.

ROW 22: With black, repeat Row 20. Turn.

ROW 23: With black, repeat Row 21. Slide.

ROW 24: With red, repeat Row 20. Break off red.
BO all sts with black.

Repeat for other wing, reversing colors, if desired, to make the second wing a mirror image of the first. Weave in ends.

Acknowledgments

One of the many rewards of knitting is the community that it fosters. For this book, I was helped by many friends, old and new. First, I must thank the designers who contributed their beautiful and innovative projects to *Weekend Knitting*, and Ericka McConnell, who took the photographs, with the help of prop stylist Loren Simons and wardrobe stylist Gerri Williams. Susi Oberhelman designed the book with her usual expertise and kindness. This is the third time we have worked together on a knitting book, and I am still hopeful that one of these days she will advance beyond her garter-stitch swatch. For technical editing, I relied on the combined geniuses of Lori Gayle and Dee Neer. Their knowledge of knitting is awe-inspiring, as are their abilities to write, understand, and clarify instructions, from the simplest to the most complex. For knitting of samples, I am grateful to Alissa Baptista, Noreen Blood, Therese Inverso, Lidia Karabinech, and Cheryl Zylla. For help finding literary quotes and knitting scenes in books and movies, I am grateful to Lorraine Ciancio, Adina Klein, Susan Lydon, Lela Nargi, Shirl the Purl, Wren Ross, and Denyse Specktor. Like so many times before, I must thank Margrit Lohrer and Albrecht Pichler for opening up beautiful Morehouse Farm for photography. Thanks are also due to all of the models: Sam Barron, Debora Cicchini, Rowan Douglass, Caitlin FitzGerald, Sadie Frost, Emily Lundberg, Shonquios Moreno, Harry Simons, Monique, Isabelle, and Anabelle King, Albrecht Pichler, Claire Raibourn, Amalia Nayeli Steinbach Sanchez, Cynthia Schmae, Jacqueline Shapiro, Annie Tirschwell, and Lola Geary Wright. Finally, I must thank Leslie Stoker, my longtime publisher, whose loyalty and confidence motivate me, and my family, with whom I plan to spend many more weekends now that this book is finished.

Contributors

PAM ALLEN
Pam is editor of *Interweave Knits* magazine and author of *Knitting for Dummies* (John Wiley & Sons). She has designed handknits for magazines and yarn companies for the past twenty years.

VÉRONIK AVERY
Véronik lives in Montreal with her husband and daughter. Formerly a costume designer and photography student, she taught herself to knit following her daughter's birth. Visit her website at www.veronikavery.com.

ALISSA BAPTISTA
Alissa taught herself to knit when she was fifteen years old. She is now a part-time freelance designer based in Saugerties, New York.

DEBBIE BLISS
Debbie has published over twenty books of handknitting designs and also produces her own line of yarns. She lives with her family in London. Visit her website at www.debbiebliss.freeserve.co.uk

ANN BUDD
Ann learned to knit at age twelve when she spent a year in Switzerland. Ann is managing editor of *Interweave Knits* magazine and author of *The Knitter's Handy Book of Patterns* (Interweave). She lives in Boulder, Colorado, with her husband and three sons.

TEVA DURHAM
Teva designs and knits in New York City. With visual artists as parents and a poet and a pianist for grandparents, Teva set out at a young age to find her metier. She studied theater and fiction and floundered about until she realized the craft that made her happiest was the knitting always at hand to "distract" her from more "serious" endeavors. She honed her technical expertise as an editor at *Vogue Knitting*, although her design approach is often to forget the "proper" way to knit a garment in order to explore new territory from a blank slate. Visit her website at www.loop-d-loop.com.

WENDY EASTON
Wendy learned to knit when she was nine years old and continued to knit throughout her childhood, her career as a commercial artist, as well as while working toward her MFA in painting and raising her children. She discovered a mentor through the books and videotapes of Elizabeth Zimmermann, as well as Meg Swansen's knitting camp and Meg's warm encouragement. She lives with her family in the Chicago area.

NICKY EPSTEIN
Nicky is one of America's leading and most prolific knitwear designers, authors, and innovators. Her work has been featured in the nation's top magazines, yarn manufacturers' catalogs, bestselling books, on television, and in museums. She is the author of *Crochet for Barbie Doll* (Soho), *Knits for Barbie Doll* (Soho), *Knitting for Your Home* (Taunton), *Nicky Epstein's Knitted Embellishments* (Interweave), and *The Knit Hat Book* (Taunton).

NORAH GAUGHAN
Norah is design director for Reynolds, Artful Yarns, and Adrienne Vittadini Yarns, divisions of JCA, Inc. Her work has appeared in myriad magazines, including *Vogue Knitting, Interweave Knits, Family Circle Easy Knitting,* and *Knitter's Magazine,* as well as in several books such as *Knitting in America* and *Vogue Knitting: American Collection.* Norah admits to being ridiculously devoted to knitting and knit design, with her greatest happiness found in success with a new technique and her greatest peace found in the realization that there will always be more to learn.

PRISCILLA A. GIBSON-ROBERTS
Priscilla is a lifelong textile enthusiast with degrees from Texas Tech University and Purdue University. She has shared her knowledge of ethnic handspinning and knitting traditions around the world through magazine articles and books, including *Knitting in the Old Way* (Nomad), *Simple Socks, Plain & Fancy* (Nomad), *High Whorling* (Nomad), *Salish Indian Sweaters* (Interweave), and *Ethnic Socks & Stockings* (XRX).

LANA HAMES
Lana enjoys designing handknits with eco-friendly and durable hemp yarns. Her fascination with hemp fiber began in the early 1990s, while studying textiles with Judith MacKenzie. She now operates Lanaknits Designs in Nelson, British Columbia. Visit her website at www.hempforknitting.com

MARGRIT LOHRER
Margrit is the co-owner—with her husband Albrecht Pichler—of Morehouse Farm, a merino sheep farm

in Milan, New York, and In Sheep's Clothing, a retail store in Rock City, New York. She learned to knit as a young child in Switzerland. The farm and shop have been featured in many publications, including *Martha Stewart Living, Victoria,* and the *New York Times,* as well as the books *Knitting in America* and *Kids Knitting.*

LUCY MACKENZIE & KIRSTEEN MITCALFE

Lucy and Kirsteen are cofounders of Pride and Joy, a Scottish mail-order source for the Pride and Joy line of traditional handknitted clothes for babies and young children. Their website is www.prideandjoyonline.com.

SHEILA MEYER

Sheila's knitting experiences began one day in the mid-1970s when she inadvertently walked into a yarn shop. This fortuitous accident led to an exciting career and worldwide travel, first with well-known American fashion companies such as Perry Ellis, Ralph Lauren, and Anne Klein, then with indigenous women in developing countries via nonprofit organizations like the International Rescue Committee and Save the Children.

ANNIE MODESITT

Annie taught herself to knit at age twenty-five. She believes that knitting can be a mind-opening experience, and works to expand the craft by creating nontraditional items. Her work has appeared in major knitting magazines as well as on Broadway, in film, and in galleries. She lives in New Jersey with her husband and two children.

DEBORAH NEWTON

Deborah resides in Providence, Rhode Island, and has been a professional knitwear designer since 1982. She sells her work to yarn companies, magazines, and the fashion industry. Her book, *Designing Knitwear* (Taunton), has been in print since 1992.

KRISTIN NICHOLAS

Kristin is a knitwear designer and decorative artist who lives with her husband and daughter on a farm in Massachusetts. She is coauthor and illustrator of *Knitting for Baby* (Stewart, Tabori & Chang), illustrator of *Kids Knitting* (Artisan), and author of *Knitting the New Classics* (Sterling) and *Knitting Today's Classics* (Lark). For sixteen years, she was creative director of Classic Elite Yarns. Her designs have been featured in many publications, including *Interweave Knits, Vogue Knitting, House and Garden,* and *Better Homes and Gardens.* Visit her website at www.kristinnicholas.com.

LINDA NIEMEYER

Inspired by a PBS documentary about alpacas, Linda quit her day job as a graphic designer, bought a pregnant alpaca, and started a herd of her own. The alpacas are now pets, but the yarn business they inspired, Blue Sky Alpacas, is going strong. Visit her website at www.blueskyalpacas.com.

LEIGH RADFORD

An award-winning graphic designer and the art director for *Interweave Knits* magazine, Leigh loves to experiment with new ways to combine fibers. Her designs appear regularly in *Interweave Knits* and have also been published by Fiber Trends and Classic Elite Yarns.

JO SHARP

Jo is a knitwear designer (and mother) living and working in the port city of Fremantle in western Australia. She began her creative career as a fine artist working in acrylic and mixed media and graduated to working with colored yarns in 1986 when she "stumbled" upon some yarn outside her local yarn store. The Jo Sharp Hand Knitting Collections, Jo's own line of yarns and patterns, now sell worldwide. Visit her website at www.josharp.com.au.

KATE SOKOLOFF

Kate knits, designs, and sings in Portland, Oregon, with her two sons. She is founder of Katharine Wheel Productions, which develops and produces events and theatrical productions throughout the Portland area. She is also producing director and performer with the Christmas Revels, where she always strives to find new reasons to knit on stage.

DENYSE SPECKTOR

Denyse learned to knit from her mother at the age of five. When her wearable art sold to Beverly Hills boutiques, she became a second-generation professional knitter. She has created handknits for films, commercials, music videos, television programming, gallery exhibition, as well as knitting magazines and yarn companies. Visit her website at www.thebigyarn.com.

CINDY TAYLOR

Cindy is a third-generation knitter. She designs for the garment industry and teaches in the fashion department at Virginia Commonwealth University. Her view of knitting is just as optimistic as her view of life, "Anything is possible." Her visual and graphic art background strongly influences her bold yet feminine creations.

Sources

Berroco
14 Elmdale Rd., PO Box 367
Uxbridge, MA 01569-0367
508-278-2527
www.berroco.com

Blue Sky Alpacas
PO Box 88
Cedar, MN 55011
888-460-8862
www.blueskyalpacas.com

Brown Sheep Company
100662 County Rd. 16
Mitchell, NE 69357
800-826-9136
www.brownsheep.com

Classic Elite Yarns
122 Western Ave.
Lowell, MA 01851
978-453-2837
www.classiceliteyarns.com

Crystal Palace Yarns
160 23rd St.
Richmond, CA 94804
510-237-9988
www.straw.com

Harrisville Designs
Center Village, PO Box 806
Harrisville, NH 03450
603-827-3333
www.harrisville.com

JCA, Inc. (Artful Yarns, Reynolds, Paternayan, Jo Sharp)
35 Scales Ln.
Townsend, MA 01469
978-597-8794
www.jcacrafts.com

KnitKnack.com
(knitting needles on page 149)
20 Sagitta Way
Coto de Caza, CA 92679
949-709-2678
www.knitknack.com

Knitting Fever, Inc. (Debbie Bliss Yarns)
PO Box 336
315 Bayview Ave.
Amityville, NY 11701
516-546-3600
www.knittingfever.com

Koigu Wool Designs
PO Box 158
Chatsworth, ON
N0H 1G0, Canada
888-765-WOOL
www.koigu.com

Lanaknits
320 Vernon St., Suite 3B
Nelson, BC
V1L 4E4, Canada
888-301-0011
www.lanaknits.com

Louet Sales
808 Commerce Park Dr.
Ogdensburg, NY 13669
631-925-4502
www.louet.com

MacIver Company
(slipper soles on page 28)
PO Box 2086
Brockton, MA 02305
508-583-2501

Mission Falls
5333 Casgrain #1204
Montreal, QC
H2T 1X3, Canada
877-244-1204
www.missionfalls.com

Morehouse Farm
141 Milan Hill Rd.
Milan, NY 12571
845-758-6493
www.morehousefarm.com

Muench Yarns, Inc.
1323 Scott St.
Petaluma, CA 94954
800-733-9276
www.muenchyarns.com

Nordic Fiber Arts (Røros Lamullgarn)
4 Cutts Rd.
Durham, NH 03824
603-868-1196
www.nordicfiberarts.com

One World Button Supply Co.
41 Union Square West, Suite 311
New York, NY 10003
212-691-1331
www.oneworldbuttons.com

Westminster Fibers (Jaeger and Rowan Yarns)
165 Ledge St.
Nashua, NH 03060
800-445-9276
www.westminsterfibers.com

Prop and Wardrobe Credits

Page 2: Lounge top from Erica Tanov, 204 Elizabeth St., New York, NY 10012; 212-334-8020.

Pages 5 and 41: Yarn from Purl, 137 Sullivan St., New York, NY 10012; 212-420-8796.

Page 47 and 61: Coats from Erica Tanov.

Page 78: Earrings from Mimi Golzer, 160 South St., 2nd floor, New York, NY 10038; 212-233-2937. Camisole and slip/skirt from Erica Tanor.

Pages 88 and 90: Earrings from Mimi Golzer.

Page 93: Skirt from Hodge Podge, 195 Chrystie St., 8th floor, New York, NY 10002; 212-533-9995.

Index